EUROPE

Germany p.16

Copenhagen, Denmark p.110

Łódź, Poland p.161

Belarus p.46

Slovenia p.169

Novi Sad, Serbia p.120

Albania p.166

Piedmont, Italy p.60

Zadar, Croatia p.148

Jordan p.34

Southern Nile Valley, Egypt p.161

Russian Far East p.84

Kyrgyzstan p.30

ASIA

Kathmandu, Nepal p.128

Bangladesh p.166

Gujarat, India p.90

Shēnzhèn, China p.116

Sri Lanka p.10

NORTH PACIFIC OCEAN

AFRICA

São Tomé & Príncipe p.50

Maldives p.163

Indonesia p.40

INDIAN OCEAN

Zimbabwe p.20

AUSTRALIA

The Red Centre, Australia p.74

SOUTHERN OCEAN

When Lonely Planet talks the rest of the world listens. That's why tourist boards all over the world await its top 10 lists with bated breath – inclusion practically guarantees a bumper year.
IRISH INDEPENDENT, IRELAND

Beautiful to look at and fun to read, Lonely Planet's roundup is a must-own.
PUBLISHERS WEEKLY, USA

As someone who loves travelling – and even the prospect of planning my next trip – this compact guide was a real treat. The sumptuous photographs alone...were enough to transport me momentarily into holiday mode.
NZ HERALD

Full of mind-blowing travel destinations, all perfectly showcasing the wonderful world around us...the guys at Lonely Planet will inspire you to get up off your bum and start the adventure of a lifetime.
FAMOUS MAGAZINE, AUSTRALIA

The annual Lonely Planet guide is packed with useful tips, fascinating facts and excellent advice.
MAIL ON SUNDAY, UK

For those suffering itchy feet, but uncertain as to which direction to point them...
OTTAWA CITIZEN, CANADA

THE LONELY PLANET STORY

WHERE IT ALL BEGAN...
A beat-up old car, a few dollars in the pocket, and a sense of adventure.

That's all Tony and Maureen Wheeler needed for the trip of a lifetime. They met on a park bench in Regent's Park, London and married a year later. For their honeymoon, they decided to attempt what few people thought possible – crossing Europe and Asia overland, all the way to Australia.

It was too amazing an experience to keep to themselves. Urged on by their friends, they stayed up nights at their kitchen table writing, typing and stapling together their very first travel guide, *Across Asia on the Cheap*.

Within a week they'd sold 1500 copies and Lonely Planet was born. Two years later, their second journey led to *South-East Asia on a Shoestring*, which led to books on Nepal, Australia, Africa and India, which led to...you get the picture.

BEST IN TRAVEL 2019

THE BEST IN TRAVEL PROMISE

Where is the best place to visit right now?

This is the most hotly contested topic at Lonely Planet and dominates more conversations than any other. As self-confessed travel geeks, our staff collectively rack up hundreds of thousands of miles each year, exploring almost every destination on the planet in the process.

Where is the best place to visit right now? We ask everyone at Lonely Planet, from our writers and editors all the way to our online family of social media influencers. And each year they come up with hundreds of places that are buzzy right now, offer new things for travellers to see or do, or are criminally overlooked and underrated.

Amid fierce debate, the list is whittled down by our panel of travel experts to just 10 countries, 10 regions, 10 cities and 10 best value destinations. Each is chosen for its topicality, unique experiences and 'wow' factor. We don't just report on the trends, we set them – helping you get there before the crowds do.

Put simply, what remains in the pages that follow is the cream of this year's travel picks, courtesy of Lonely Planet: 10 countries, 10 regions, 10 cities, 10 best value destinations and a host of travel lists to inspire you to explore for yourself.

So what are you waiting for?

70

144

20

CONTENTS

LONELY PLANET'S

TOP 10
COUNTRIES

Sri Lanka / Germany / Zimbabwe / Panama / Kyrgyzstan
Jordan / Indonesia / Belarus / São Tomé & Príncipe / Belize

SRI LANKA

▬▬ Sri Lanka is decidedly having its moment in the equatorial sun and change is coming swiftly. Already notable to intrepid travellers for its mix of religions and cultures, its timeless temples, its rich and accessible wildlife, its growing surf scene and its people who defy all odds by their welcome and friendliness after decades of civil conflict, this is a country revived. There's now more than ever for families, adrenaline junkies, eco-tourists, wellness seekers and foodies of all budgets. Even the north and east, including areas previously off limits, difficult to reach or lacking in services, deliver new discoveries.

Statues of
Buddha in
Isurumuniya
Rock Temple
in Anuradhapura

© EFFESENKO / SHUTTERSTOCK

11

Population: 21.2 million

Capital: Colombo

Languages: Sinhalese, Tamil (official), English (spoken)

Unit of currency: Sri Lankan rupee

How to get there: As Sri Lanka is an island with no sea link, Bandaranaike International Airport, north of Colombo, is the primary port of entry for all arrivals, with many nonstop flights from Asia, the Middle East and Europe.

'If you want relaxing and calm, Sri Lanka is the place to live, to visit. Its laidback, Buddhist-influenced, island mentality means we do things cool.'

Dileep Mudadeniya, vice president at Cinnamon Hotels & Resorts

TELL ME MORE...

In 2015, renovated rails carried train services to Jaffna in the north for the first time since 1990, while brand-new controlled-access expressways have drastically reduced travel times to the south as far as Matara (with more routes to come). And scheduled and charter domestic flights now speed travellers between most major cities. This improved transport network has opened up tourism in Sri Lanka in ways hardly imaginable 10 years ago. Destinations that once required determination and endurance to reach are now a comfortable ride away. Just as more people are reaching more places throughout the island, so too are an increasing number of quality hotels, restaurants, sustainable tour operators and diverse experiences meeting rising needs. Opportunities for expanded

ITINERARY
Three weeks in Sri Lanka

• Stroll through Pettah, **Colombo**'s thronging main market, to get familiar with the mix of Sinhalese, Tamil and Muslim cultures.

• Spend a few days mesmerised by the 1000-year-old ruins of Buddhist fortresses and cities in the **Cultural Triangle**.

• Attend a colourful and cacophonous *puja* (religious ritual) at the clifftop Koneswaram Kovil in **Trincomalee**.

• Reserve a seat in the observation car for one of the world's most scenic rail journeys, through upcountry tea plantations from **Kandy** to **Ella**.

• After beach time and water sports at **Hikkaduwa** or Unawatuna, walk the fortified walls surrounding the colonial old town of **Galle**.

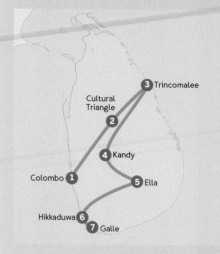

Crossing the Demodara
Nine Arches Bridge, or
'Bridge in the sky', near Ella

exploration abound – water sports, surfing and whale watching; jungle hikes, safaris and other nature-based experiences; cooking lessons and village homestays; and yoga retreats and Ayurveda centres.

UNMISSABLE EXPERIENCES

• Storied biodiversity finds shelter in protected natural areas covering more than 25% of the island. National park wildlife highlights include Minneriya's annual gathering of 300-plus elephants (July to October), the elusive leopards of Yala and the birds of Udawalawe.

• Ancient Buddhist monuments dot the central Cultural Triangle – Sigiriya, Polonnaruwa, Anuradhapura and Dambulla are Unesco World Heritage sites, as is Kandy's Temple of the Tooth. Venerable Hindu temples, such as Jaffna's sense-rousing Nallur Kandaswamy Kovil, also make for significant places to visit.

• The Hill Country's horizon-filling tea plantations are best appreciated on a scenic train trip, leisurely hike or from a wellness centre.

TIME YOUR VISIT

Generally, coastal and flatland areas are hot, while the uplands remain more temperate. Two separate monsoons – the Yala from the southwest (May–August) and the Mala from the northeast (October–January) – mean that rain is usually falling somewhere while it's warm and dry elsewhere. High season lasts from December to March.

• By Ethan Gelber

Surf's up at Narigama beach
in Hikkaduwa, a traditional
Sri Lankan village turned
popular beach resort

GERMANY

Germany has long been a powerhouse of innovation and has bestowed upon the world the printing press, the automobile, the aspirin and other milestones of invention. And 100 years ago, a little school in the Thuringian countryside kick-started an aesthetic movement so globally influential that its reverberations are still felt today: the Bauhaus. Join the year-long birthday party of this midwife of modernism that was founded in Weimar in 1919, flourished in Dessau and was quashed by the Nazis in Berlin in 1933. Sparkling new museums are set to open in these three cities along with scores of related events and exhibitions held throughout Germany.

Reconstructed Bauhaus Masters' Houses in Dessau

Population: 82.6 million

Capital: Berlin

Language: German

Unit of currency: Euro

How to get there: Germany's main international airports are Frankfurt and Munich but there are smaller ones in Berlin, Hamburg, Düsseldorf, Cologne, Stuttgart and numerous other cities. Trains and buses link the country with other destinations throughout Europe.

TELL ME MORE...

A visit to Germany will plunge you into a stirring alchemy of tradition and vision. Like Atlas carrying the world on his shoulders, the muscular Alps in the south hoist up a country where scaling a mountain, holing up in a medieval castle, cycling through wine country or knocking back beers in a cosy pub are all equally worthy pursuits. You'll be moved just by standing still in places where great minds such as Beethoven, Einstein, Goethe or Marx lived and worked. Urban nomads, meanwhile, should train their compass on Berlin, the ever-energetic German capital, which this year will mark the 30th anniversary of the Peaceful Revolution that brought down the Berlin Wall. Tap into Germany's other flagship cities such as Hamburg, Cologne, Frankfurt

'**Germany is a cultural mecca filled with edgy and unexpected experiences, especially in my hometown of Berlin. The feeling of freedom to pursue whatever you want here is unbeatable.**'

Henrik Tidefjärd, owner of lifestyle tour agency Berlinagenten

King Ludwig II's Schloss Neuschwanstein in the Bavarian mountains

ITINERARY
Two weeks in Germany

- Feast your ears on the sounds of **Hamburg** at the city's dazzling new Elbphilharmonie concert hall.
- Peel away **Berlin**'s party layers one club at a time in this 'capital of the lost weekend'.
- Raise a birthday toast to the Bauhaus on a pilgrimage to the new museums in **Dessau** and **Weimar**.
- Enjoy **Munich** while sober by sampling canvas candy in its art museums, cheering on the legendary FC Bayern football team or gearing up for a spin around the BMW museum.
- Romance the **Rhine** on a leisurely boat trip past medieval castles, steep vineyards and half-timbered fairy-tale villages.

and Munich. Although each flaunts a distinctive personality, all are united by a fierce dedication to cultural, culinary and historical delights. Germany is here to charm, enlighten and surprise you.

UNMISSABLE EXPERIENCES

- Clamber around the wildly romantic rockscapes of Saxon Switzerland, a national park near Dresden, where one almost expects hobbits to hide among the otherworldly sandstone formations, moss-draped ravines and damp caves.
- Journey into the mind of Ludwig II, if not at his tourist-drowned Schloss Neuschwanstein then at the petite Schloss Linderhof where the 'Mad King' retreated to. Marvel at such excesses as a conch-shaped boat, a jewel-encrusted bedroom and his frilly peacock throne.
- Savour fine Rieslings and other classic German wines along the serpentine Mosel River, clapping eyes on ancient Roman monuments, medieval castles, Europe's steepest vineyard and endearing half-timbered villages en route.

TIME YOUR VISIT

Germany is a year-round destination, although most visitors arrive between May and September when the weather is pleasant, days are long and the festival season is in full swing. The best winter month is December, when Christmas markets brighten town squares. Ski season hits its peak in January and February.

- By Andrea Schulte-Peevers

The awe-inspiring
cascade of
Victoria Falls

03

ZIMBABWE

While it may be known for making the headlines for all the wrong reasons, Zimbabwe has always been a country that travellers on the ground have raved about. Not only is it one of Africa's safest destinations, it's one blessed with ultra-friendly locals, Big Five–filled national parks, World Heritage–listed archaeological ruins, forested mountains and, of course, the mighty Victoria Falls. And for the first time in recent memory, Zimbabweans are looking to the future with a concrete sense of hope and a renewed optimism of what is possible. The excitement following the end of Robert Mugabe's time in power is palpable in the air and in the warm welcome from locals looking to a new dawn.

Elephants in Hwange National Park, Zimbabwe's largest reserve

Population: 16.2 million

Capital: Harare

Languages: Shona, Ndebele, English and 13 other official local dialects

Units of currency: US dollar, Zimbabwean bond notes, South African rand

How to get there: Both Harare and Victoria Falls have international airports that are served by flights from across Africa and Europe, and Dubai. For overlanders there are border crossings with South Africa, Zambia, Botswana and Mozambique.

TELL ME MORE...

Although Zimbabweans have endured nearly two decades of hardships, economic failure and political violence, they've never stopped welcoming visitors with warmth and unmatched hospitality. That will still be the case in 2019, when you'll also get the chance to ride the wave of excitement as they collectively work to recalibrate and right the good ship Zimbabwe.

During your stay you'll journey through diverse landscapes and take in varied experiences, ones to be enjoyed as much by nature lovers as those into art, culture and history. One day you could be lazing on a houseboat drinking beers in Kariba, eyeing a leopard on safari or exploring archaeological sites; and the next you might be bungee jumping at Vic Falls or trekking through the pristine hills of the Eastern Highlands. Despite its underdog status, Zimbabwe is a country that is sure to leave a lasting impression, through both its beauty and strength of character.

UNMISSABLE EXPERIENCES

• Nowhere is more synonymous with Zimbabwe than the World Heritage–listed Victoria Falls. This blockbuster sight (known locally as Mosi-oa-Tunya; the 'smoke that thunders') has been drawing tourists by the bucketload for generations, here to witness one of the world's most famous natural wonders at full power. It also harbours a world-class adventure scene, from white-water rafting on Grade V rapids along the Zambezi River, to bungee jumping off its iconic bridge, to chopper rides over the falls.

• Another big lure to Zimbabwe is its national parks, each featuring unique and dramatic scenic landscapes and ample opportunity to spot all of Africa's celebrity animals, including all five of the Big Five (lion, leopard, buffalo, elephant and rhino).

> **'Quartz crystal mountains, waterfalls, caves, gold, diamonds and African time: Chimanimani is blessed with natural beauty and it's home to the chronically groovy of Zimbabwe. I also love that it has no mosquitoes!'**
>
> *Allen Radford, owner of Heaven Lodge, Chimanimani*

TIME YOUR VISIT

Although Zimbabwe is a year-round destination, to experience its perfect 25°C sunshine with blazing blue skies, aim to visit between April and October. For white-water purists, the rafting season peaks in August. For Victoria Falls, the best panoramas are viewed around July, or come February to May after the region's summer rains if you want to experience the falls' full impact.

• By Trent Holden

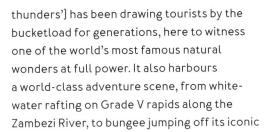

ITINERARY
Two weeks in Zimbabwe

• Take in Zimbabwe's laidback capital, **Harare**, with its museums, galleries, fleamarkets and cosmopolitan restaurants.

• Take a walk on the really wild side in **Mana Pools National Park** for thrilling, up-close animal encounters.

• Experience the mystique of the World Heritage–listed **Great Zimbabwe**, an 11th-century archaeological site that remains the symbolic heart of the nation.

• Explore the colonial architecture of **Bulawayo**, then drop into nearby **Matobo National Park** – home to rhinos and rock art.

• Drop by **Hwange National Park** to witness its massive elephant herds.

• Take in the majestic **Victoria Falls** at full bore, before grabbing a paddle to tame some Grade V rapids.

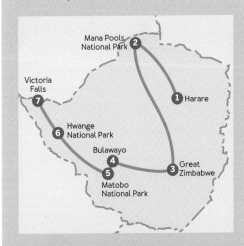

The Great Zimbabwe ruins
date to the 11th century

PANAMA

▰▰▰ **Welcome to the crossroads of the Americas.** In Panama, north meets south in a fiesta of tropical biodiversity, celebrated at the world-class BioMuseo. East meets West through expanding world trade, with the world's biggest cargo ships travelling the recently revamped Panama Canal. Darling Panama packs so many treasures into one small country – from white-sand beaches to tropical rainforests, misty highlands and indigenous culture – it is shocking that it's somehow still under the radar. In 2019, Panama City pledges to party like never before, marking its 500-year history with one raucous jubilee that you won't want to miss.
¡Viva Panama!

Colourful coral reefs off
Bocas del Toro on Panama's
Caribbean coast

04

PANAMA

Population: 4 million

Capital: Panama City

Language: Spanish

Unit of currency: US dollar (known as the balboa in Panama)

How to get there: Most international arrivals go to Tocumen International Airport in Panama City, but it's also possible to arrive at Aeropuerto Enrique Malek in David, handy to the highlands and Pacific coast.

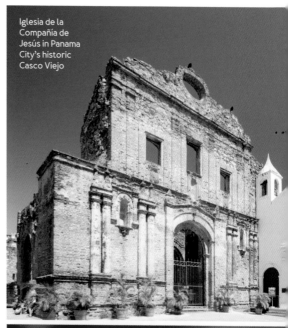
Iglesia de la Compañía de Jesús in Panama City's historic Casco Viejo

TELL ME MORE...

Although there's a thrill to plying the locks of the Panama Canal, this country is much more than the world's greatest shortcut. Panama's simple pleasures start with burrowing your bare feet into powdery sand, frosty lager in hand. From the verdant Caribbean to big Pacific swells, Panama's rich coastal offerings span from the stilted bungalows of Bocas del Toro to the postcard islets of the indigenous region of Guna Yala. Head inland to explore rainforest that's largely untrammelled by visitors, studied intently by scientists and prowled by big cats, monkeys and toucans. Though adventure never lies far off, the nationwide talent for chilling out can be highly contagious. Annual polls have consistently ranked Panama as one of the happiest countries in the world. And why not? People are easygoing, the sun is high and the water's warm. Soon you won't be drinking that ice-cold Balboa beer alone.

A poison dart frog on Isla Bastimentos

UNMISSABLE EXPERIENCES

• Dive and snorkel the underwater paradise of Parque Nacional Coiba. Once an island prison for notorious criminals, this pristine, isolated

ITINERARY
Ten days in Panama

- Explore the cobblestone streets of **Panama City's** Casco Viejo, with its crumbling convents, hip bars and the city's finest restaurants housed in colonial wonders.
- Take in the enormity of the mighty **Panama Canal** at the Miraflores Locks or take a kayak tour on Lago Gatun where megaships sail in the distance.
- Soak up the Caribbean flavour of **Bocas del Toro** by snorkelling the rainbow reefs and searching for tiny red frogs.
- Tour the lush coffee estates of **Boquete** in the misty highlands.
- Party like a local in the tradition-rich **Península de Azuero**, which has a beautiful coastline and many colonial villages rife with festivals.

04 BEST IN TRAVEL 2019

Pacific park shelters manta rays, seahorses, schools of colourful fish, whale sharks and scarlet macaws. Visitors can also hike through primary rainforest to spot wild scarlet macaws and howler monkeys.

- Indulge in a tropical gourmet feast in Panama City. Ranked among the world's best restaurants, tiny eatery Donde José pays homage to Panama's diverse cultures by using regional ingredients such as cashews and chayote (a type of squash) in fusion dishes created with delicious artistry.
- Explore Afro-Caribbean culture at the Festival de Diablos y Congos. Held in February or March, Portobelo's biannual fete re-enacts a colonial slave rebellion with vibrant music, drumming and street dancing.

'My favourite thing about Panama is that it's an international country in terms of the history and the way people view things. It's infused by so many different elements.'
Ryan Stacy, boutique hotel owner

TIME YOUR VISIT
January's Jazzfest has music seeping from the sidewalks of Panama City. Celebrations for Panama City's 500 years will hit fever pitch on the capital's 15 August anniversary. In early November, millions of migratory birds of prey soar over the capital. Rainy season varies by region, but most visitors land between December and March.

- By Carolyn McCarthy

Köl-Tör lake is
set amid supreme
mountain terrain

05

05
BEST IN TRAVEL 2019

KYRGYZSTAN

Kyrgyzstan's moment on the world tourism stage seems to have come following huge buzz from the 2018 World Nomad Games, Central Asia's competition dedicated to its traditional (and quirky) regional sports. The time to visit has never been better – more than 2700km of newly marked trekking routes; a countrywide push of community-run tour products; a revamped national highway system cutting transit times immensely; and a simplified e-visa programme for those not on the list of 60+ visa-free countries – but do it now: Kyrgyzstan is quickly becoming an in-the-know favourite for independent travellers seeking unspoilt natural beauty.

Population: 5.8 million
Capital: Bishkek
Languages: Kyrgyz, Russian
Unit of currency: Kyrgyz som
How to get there: Kyrgyzstan's main international airport in Bishkek welcomes the majority of international visitors, mostly connecting to Istanbul and Moscow, whereas more intrepid travellers arrive overland on Silk Road journeys from the neighbouring 'stans and China.

TELL ME MORE...

Long off the tourism radar, Central Asia is finally getting the attention it deserves, and Kyrgyzstan is at the heart of that growth. World-class mountain landscapes abound, and nearly every little valley offers up a sparkling lake or panoramic pass for explorers who make the effort. The country's long-standing nomadic traditions, resurgent in a big way

'When I'm away from Kyrgyzstan I miss the mountain views, the friendliness and hospitality of our people, the ability to show up at absolutely any time to a friend's house and be welcomed – something that often feels as if it's missing in other cultures.'

Gulmira Myrzakmat, Bishkek resident

since the end of Soviet-era collectivisation, the shockingly beautiful landscapes and soothing sense of hospitality combine for an unforgettable experience.

Though it's the nature that will bring you in, it's the intoxicating diversity of cultural

ITINERARY
Three weeks in Kyrgyzstan

- In leafy **Bishkek**, visit the renovated National Historical Museum then explore the burgeoning coffee-shop and craft-beer scenes.
- Travel east to trekking-hub **Karakol**, exploring the city's multi-ethnic heritage at the Dungan Family Dinner.
- Take on the **Ak-Suu Transverse**, a seven-day, 115km trek past stunning panoramas of remote lakes and snowy peaks, ending in eco-tourism village **Jyrgalan**.
- From Kochkor or Jumgal, hire a horse to ride up to vast **Son-Köl** lake to relax at the shore-side yurt camps.
- Finish in Silk Road city **Osh**, combining its local bazaars and amazing food with the Osh Plov Journey.

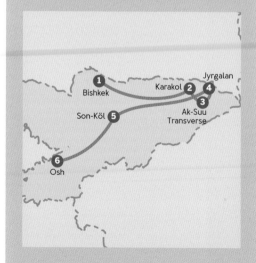

traditions that will bring you back. Ethnic communities from across Eurasia call Kyrgyzstan home – the mix of languages, cuisines, costumes and traditions give insight into a modern community every bit as vibrant as the ancient Silk Road. From a Kyrgyz *toi* to an Uzbek wedding or a local village festival, Kyrgyzstan is a place of celebrations just waiting to welcome visitors.

UNMISSABLE EXPERIENCES

• By foot, on horseback or atop a mountain bike, however you decide to go, get out into the massive mountains of the Pamir-Alay and Tien-Shan ranges to see what the fuss over these 'Celestial Mountains' is all about.

• Overnight in a yurt, the felt tent of Kyrgyz nomads, whether at luxury tourist camps on the south shore of Lake Issyk-Köl or up in the mountains at a working shepherd's camp.

• Seek out Salburuun, a centuries-old partnership in which local trainers and their golden eagles work together to hunt wild game and protect livestock herds from wolves.

TIME YOUR VISIT

Head into the mountains from June to October to explore the country's landscapes and get a glimpse of those nomadic traditions and yurt-camp life. In between hikes and horse treks, take a day to catch one of the almost-weekly community-based tourism festivals held throughout the country during the months of July and August.

• By Stephen Lioy

Selling Central Asian bread in the bazaars of Osh

JORDAN

▬ Have a taste for adventure? Here's a new recipe: find a path 650km long and set aside 36 days (42 with rest stops) to hike it; throw in a mindblowing Rift Valley landscape crumpled with canyons and made green after flash floods; add vistas of the lowest point on Earth (the Dead Sea) and of biblical catastrophe (Sodom); season with wildflowers strewn over crusader castles; combine with a healthy pinch of irrepressible Jordanian optimism and there you have it – the Jordan Trail, the country's latest signature dish. Be ahead of the pack to sample the highs and lows of this epic route.

The Treasury (Al Khazneh), carved out of the rock in magical ancient Petra

Population: 10 million

Capital: Amman

Languages: Arabic (official), English (spoken)

Unit of currency: Jordanian dinar

How to get there: Jordan's international airport is a 45-minute bus ride south of the capital. Other points of entry are by ferry from Nuweiba in Egypt to Jordan's southern city of Aqaba or overland from Israel and the Palestinian Territories.

TELL ME MORE...

Ever since 27-year-old explorer JL Burckhardt rediscovered Petra for the Western world in 1812, travellers have commented on the quality of adventure offered in this ancient land. Whether digging up the past in the ruined cities of the Roman Decapolis or tracing Moses' route to Mt Nebo for a view of the Promised Land, exciting endeavours are a Jordan speciality. Now the country has given exploration a modern twist by making it easier than ever to engage sustainably with its beautiful landscapes. Not only does the newly introduced Jordan Pass (from JD70) offer a free visa and access to the country's main sites, including Petra, but there's also a new Bike Trail complementing the Jordan Trail (opened in 2017), desert safaris at Shaumari Wildlife Reserve and off-road routes snaking across the desolate Badia. Add in canyoning, rock-climbing and Red Sea diving, and Jordan is arguably the activities hub of the region.

UNMISSABLE EXPERIENCES

• Amble at first light through the Siq (canyon) in the ancient city of Petra to behold the rock-cut Treasury in the first sunbeams of the day. Continue through the sandstone labyrinth

'I was born in a Bedouin tent, raised by traditions passed through my family for centuries. The desert offers a sanctuary of true peace and I thank God that I live here.'

Ahmed Oqlah Al Zalabeyh, owner of Rum Stars Camp, Wadi Rum

Fireside at one of Wadi Rum's Bedouin camps

of cliffs and tombs of this world-class site to Petra's magical High Places.

- Float 430m below sea level in the skin-smartingly salty Dead Sea. Relax, after the effort of staying upright in mega-buoyancy, at a spa in the area's pleasure dome resorts.
- Go eye-to-eye with eagles at Dana Biosphere Reserve on a leg of the Jordan Trail – one of the world's best hikes.

TIME YOUR VISIT

Encompassing different climatic zones, Jordan can be visited year-round, with Red Sea diving at its best in winter (November to February), hiking from March to April and canyoning in September and October before the rains begin. Jordan's top sites are open but more of a challenge in the fearsome heat of summer.

- By Jenny Walker

Catching up on the news in the Dead Sea

ITINERARY
Two weeks in Jordan

- Hike with the soap-makers of **Ajloun,** Jordan's growing hub of community tourism, near the Roman ruins of Jerash.
- Meet the locals (oryx, onager and ostrich) on safari at the newly reopened **Shaumari Wildlife Reserve.**
- In **Wadi Rum,** camp with the Bedouin in a landscape loved by Lawrence (of Arabia).
- Trace the path of history along the King's Highway from the hidden 'pink city' of **Petra** to the mosaic-making town of **Madaba.**

The vast desert landscape of Wadi Rum has served as the setting for numerous Hollywood films

The volcanic lake of Segara Anak viewed from Mt Rinjani

07 BEST IN TRAVEL 2019

INDONESIA

▬▬▬▬ **Indonesia is as diverse as its span is long,** from new eco-resorts offering orang-utan encounters in Sumatra to the tribal traditions of Papua. More than 17,000 islands make up the medley of cultures, cuisines and religions across the archipelago, offering a kaleidoscope of experience. Thanks to substantial investment in new air, land and sea connections, it has never been easier to explore this tropical country. Nationals of 169 countries were granted visa-free access in 2016, meaning that Indonesia is embracing visitors to all its far-flung corners. Now is the ideal time to explore before all its secrets are uncovered.

INDONESIA

Population: 261.1 million

Capital: Jakarta

Language: Bahasa Indonesia
(with more than 300 regional dialects)

Unit of currency: Indonesian Rupiah

How to get there: Jakarta and Bali are the main long-haul international airports; Lombok, Yogyakarta, Medan, Surabaya and Makassar offer limited regional international air connections. Boat routes provide alternative entries from Malaysia and Singapore.

TELL ME MORE...

Indonesia, with its tropical climate and location along the Pacific Ring of Fire, is stealing the limelight from its more-traversed neighbour nations. You can witness otherworldly blue sulphur 'flames' at the Ijen volcano complex, hike among wildlife-rich rainforests in Kalimantan and Sumatra, or explore Raja Ampat, a collection of remote islands where lapping waves, star-studded skies and endemic birds are your only distractions. Jakarta and Bali are leading the way in fusion cuisine and lavish bars, but luxury is no longer confined to major destinations. Glitzy liveaboards, such as *Tiger Blue*, now ply the archipelago, allowing divers to discover the rich marine life in comfort, while Labuan Bajo, gateway to Komodo National Park, welcomed its first five-star hotel in 2018. Traditional culture is happily still centre-stage, from the unique funeral traditions of the Toraja people to the Hindu offerings in Bali. Indonesia's new accessibility offers a multitude of adventures.

UNMISSABLE EXPERIENCES

• Discover Balinese Hinduism at the island's cultural capital, Ubud, where traditional Kecak

ITINERARY
Two weeks in Indonesia

• Trek through the forest of North Sumatra in **Gunung Leuser National Park**, where patience will be rewarded with elephant and orang-utan encounters.

• Take a flight to Yogyakarta and marvel at the vast **Borobudur** (Buddhist) and **Prambanan** (Hindu) temple complexes.

• The beaches of Lombok provide remote relaxation before you tackle the three-day hike up Indonesia's second-largest volcano, **Mt Rinjani**.

• Travel by boat to the Hindu island of **Bali**, where glitzy hotels, new wineries and an ever-evolving food scene complement traditional temples and fishing villages.

• Dive into the clear waters of **Komodo National Park** for unforgettable scuba diving alongside manta rays, before coming face-to-face with the formidable Komodo dragon.

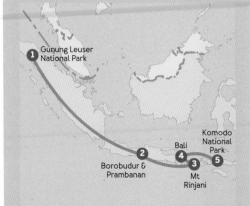

Dance, ornate water temples and daily incense-infused offerings create a spiritual setting.

• Explore the unique underwater world of Raja Ampat, a remote and captivating archipelago off West Papua's coast, and one of the world's greatest epicentres of marine biodiversity.

• Witness sunrise over Mt Bromo, an active volcano on Java, the country's largest island, before crossing the space-like 'sea of sand' to climb to the caldera and marvel at the bubbling sulphur playing behind the smoke.

TIME YOUR VISIT

Due to micro-climates across the islands, the weather is highly variable. As a general rule, the shoulder months of May, June and September provide dry, non-humid days with fewer tourists. The best diving takes place between April and October. Manta rays are most common during the wet season, from December to February.

• By Daniel James Clarke

A fearsome Komodo dragon prowls the island from which it gets its name

'I love taking trips from Jakarta to explore Indonesia's incredible nature. My favourites are to Raja Ampat in West Papua, Lake Toba in North Sumatra and Komodo Island in Flores.' *Marleen M, Jakarta resident*

Performing
traditional
dance in Bali

BELARUS

Long a beacon for those seeking the obscure, Belarus has quietly become cool on the back of relaxed visa requirements, a sneaky-good art and cafe scene, and locals who party like it's 1999. Minsk is the hub and where you must arrive and depart to take advantage of a newish five-day visa-free regime. In its impeccably restored Old Town, centred around the graceful *ratusha* (town hall), evening revellers erupt out of *bierstubes* and fashionable cocktail bars to join raucous summer street parties. Minsk has also become a hub for global events and summits. Next up: the 2019 European Games.

Cathedral of the Holy Spirit is a landmark of the Belarusian capital, Minsk

08

Population: 9.5 million
Capital: Minsk
Languages: Belarusian, Russian
Unit of currency: Belarusian rouble
How to get there: The national carrier, Belavia, and
a few Western airlines serve Minsk from Europe. Be
careful: if you fly via Russia you'll need a Russian
visa. Overland travel is possible from Ukraine,
Lithuania and Poland.

TELL ME MORE...

The buzz around Belarus rests on its edgy
frontier vibe – it has been the least touristy
country in Europe for decades. That is
changing as entry requirements ease. In 2018,
10-day visa-free regimes were introduced in
the western regions of Brest and Hrodna. Best

> 'Figuratively speaking, the heart
> of Minsk is its lungs – the parks.
> My favourite is the park by the
> Minsk Opera House.'

Minsk-born poet Valzhyna Mort

visited overland from Poland, these are rare
Europeanised nooks in Belarus. In the history-
rich city of Brest, easy-going, approachable
locals saunter along pedestrianised streets
lined with open-air cafes that beckon you
to plop down and enjoy some of Europe's
cheapest beer. The rest of the country is
more Sovietised; it's not for nothing that
Belarus is often described as a living museum
of all things Soviet. Though that's becoming
less true as the country opens up, even
Minsk, despite its charming Old Town, is best
known for its war museums and monumental

ITINERARY
Five days in Belarus

- Be dwarfed by the Stalinist architecture of
Minsk's main drag, praspekt Nezalezhnastsi
(Independence Ave), where the KGB building
lurks and Lenin statues linger.
- Take a half-day trip out of Minsk to **Khatyn**,
a moving memorial to a village obliterated
by the Nazis; it's essential to understanding
Belarus' unspeakable suffering in WWII.
- Combine **Mir Castle** with a trip to **Nyasvizh
Castle**. Built by Lithuanian nobles in the 16th
century, its lovely interiors exhibit the finest
of tsarist palace architecture.
- Look out for rare European bison in
Belavezhskaya Pushcha National Park, best
done as a day trip out of **Brest**.

Walking under a socialist star on the way to the Brest Fortress, the *Courage* monument in the background

© ALEX SKROBOT / 500PX

architecture – a tradition faithfully upheld by the country's controversial, hockey-playing president, Alexander Lukashenko.

UNMISSABLE EXPERIENCES

• Venture 90 minutes outside Minsk to the impossibly photogenic 16th-century Mir Castle, its five animated turrets reflected in an adjoining pond. The courtyard assumes a carnival atmosphere at weekends, and is a perfect place to take in lute-infused national music and sample *kvas* (a fermented wheat beverage) and *draniki* (potato pancakes).
• Ironically, Europeanised Brest is home to Belarus' most Soviet icon: *Courage*, a mammoth statue that CNN put on a list of the world's ugliest monuments (you'll either strongly agree or strongly disagree). It occupies Brest Fortress, where a band of soldiers became Soviet legends for resisting the Nazis in WWII.

TIME YOUR VISIT

Escape tourist hordes elsewhere in Europe by visiting in the summer, which is also when Minsk's street-centric nightlife is at its best. Don't miss the country-wide Kupalle Festival (6 July), a pagan tradition that involves much singing, dancing and jumping over fires.
• By Greg Bloom

The 668m-high
Pico Cão Grande
rock tower on São
Tomé Island

09

TOP 10 COUNTRIES

SÃO TOMÉ & PRÍNCIPE

From Captain Cook to Captain Kirk, explorers (both real and fictional) have always searched out places to boldly go where no one has gone before. This is your chance. The two-island nation of São Tomé & Príncipe – found floating in the Gulf of Guinea – is now calling. Be the first to hear it. Surreal landscapes climb dramatically to the heavens, jungles consume relics of the sugar, slave, cocoa and coffee trade, and tropical waters kiss its empty beaches. And whether trekking through the forests, climbing the mountains or snorkelling in the waters offshore, you'll discover many untold treasures here.

'I live in the midst of nature, and the continuous search for balance between plantation and forest excites me deeply. The views I have every day are always new.'

Claudio Corallo,
coffee and
chocolate producer

Enjoying the warm coastal waters off Príncipe

Population: 200,000
Capital: São Tomé (city)
Languages: Portuguese and Forro Creole
Unit of currency: Dobra (Db)
How to get there: São Tomé International Airport (TMS) welcomes limited flights from Europe and Africa. TAP Air Portugal links the island to Lisbon and Accra, whereas TAAG Angola Airlines connects Luanda, and Afrijet serves Libreville.

TELL ME MORE...

Nature is the ultimate lure here, especially on Príncipe, the smaller of the country's two major islands. Its dense forest canopy provides shelter for unique species of birds and plants, and is so rich in biodiversity that the entire island was named a Unesco World Biosphere Reserve in 2013. Príncipe's beaches are world-class too and, thanks to some philanthropic investment (tied to marine conservation, the biosphere reserve and

sustainable tourism), there are now a few small-scale lodges located near some of the remote stretches of sand.

The crumbling *roças* (plantations) and colonial buildings in the larger towns of both islands are also of interest, as are the São Toméans. The former tell of a different time and provide insight into the nation's economic hardships since independence from Portugal in 1975. Meanwhile, the São Toméans themselves are a picture of spirit, remaining upbeat and peaceful, with their *leve leve* ('easy easy') attitude pervading throughout.

UNMISSABLE EXPERIENCES

• Stand-up paddleboarding across the turquoise waters of Baía das Agulhas, where you'll look back to the staggering skyline composed of massive rock towers climbing from the lush shores of Príncipe.

The islands have a history of coffee production

© JUSTIN FOULKES / LONELY PLANET

ITINERARY
Two weeks in São Tomé & Príncipe

- After spending a night in **São Tomé** (city), fly to Príncipe and rest your head at **Bom Bom Resort** – where you can sort a boat or paddleboard trip to Baía das Agulhas.
- Move on to **Roça Belo Monte** for a stay at this old plantation – it's a short walk to Praia Banana and you can also organise quad bike tours here.
- Glamp next to the beach and under the stars in **Makaira Lodge**'s safari tents before flying back to São Tomé.
- Ascend **Pico de São Tomé**, the country's most famous climb.
- With your legs primed, tackle the two-day **Volta a Ilha** trek along the southwest coast.

- Gazing over Praia Banana and then trying to contain your excitement as you walk down to its golden sands, swaying palms and crystal-clear waters for some lazing, swimming, snorkelling and kayaking.
- Spending two days trekking through steep sections of jungle, over fallen trees and along winding trails (and a night camping near the summit), to reach the top of Pico de São Tomé (2024m), the island nation's highest point.

TIME YOUR VISIT
The southwest of São Tomé and Príncipe islands can be wet, particularly between October and May, while the northeast of both isles tends to be dry due to micro-climates. Temperatures generally hover below 30°C year-round. June to September is best for trekking as the ground should be dry underfoot.
- By Matt Phillips

Bom Bom Resort **2**
Roça Belo Monte **3**
Makaira Lodge **4**

Pico de São Tomé **5** **1** São Tomé

6 Volta a Ilha

BELIZE

Its Caribbean coast is fringed by the world's second-largest barrier reef; its interior is riddled with some of the most extensive and accessible cave systems in Central America; and its people are an exotic mix of Maya, Mestizo, Garifuna, Creole, Mennonite and expats. Yet many travellers struggle to place Belize on the map. However, the tide is turning. The government is moving to fully protect its unique marine environment, new eco-resorts are taking advantage of the country's stunning cayes and jungle hideaways, and travellers are discovering a slice of Central America that's relatively untouristed, safe and tantalisingly easy to reach. Get here before the inevitable crowds do.

An extraordinary sinkhole and diving hotspot, Blue Hole plunges 124m

10

A loggerhead
sea turtle in the
waters off Belize

© PNIESEN / GETTY IMAGES

© SIMON DANNHAUER / GETTY IMAGES

Population: 370,000

Capital: Belmopan

Language: English (official), Spanish, Kriol and Maya languages (spoken)

Unit of currency: Belize dollar

How to get there: Philip Goldson International Airport, 18km from Belize City, is the entry point for flights, but many travellers enter Belize overland from Mexico (usually via Chetumal from Cancun) or Guatemala. Public boats also sail to Belize from Mexico, Guatemala and Honduras.

TELL ME MORE...

Apart from that marvellous Caribbean coastline, Belize shares borders with Mexico and Guatemala. And though it's known to passing cruise-ship passengers, discerning backpackers, scuba-diving enthusiasts and eco-tourists, the country has largely remained out of the limelight.

The beauty of Belize lies in how much it packs into its small frame. Sure, you can spend time in blissed-out beach mode, sea-kayaking around the atolls and diving or snorkelling

ITINERARY
One to two weeks in Belize

- Take the boat from **Belize City** to party capital **San Pedro** on Ambergris Caye, or the more laidback **Caye Caulker**. Both offer beaches, bars and a base for diving the Blue Hole or myriad other superb sites.
- Make your way to **San Ignacio** in Cayo District, the perfect base for visiting ATM Cave, Caracol, Xunantunich, Barton Cave and more.
- Head to relaxed, beachy **Hopkins** to see the best of Garifuna drumming, then spend the day hiking in search of jaguars at **Cockscomb Basin Wildlife Sanctuary.**
- Follow the spit of coast to **Placencia**, a burgeoning beach community that's still way more relaxed than San Pedro.

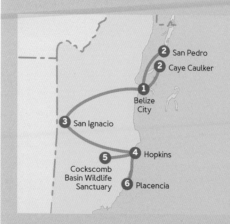

2 San Pedro
2 Caye Caulker
1 Belize City
3 San Ignacio
4 Hopkins
5 Cockscomb Basin Wildlife Sanctuary
6 Placencia

10
BEST IN TRAVEL
2019

The remains of the Maya citadel at Lamanai

'Belize, for me, is a delicious soul soup. It's a diverse harmony of cultures and beautiful blue seas blended with amazing flora and fauna. It's a great place to energise your soul.'

Daniel Velazquez, artist and owner of Soul Project Café, San Ignacio

the impossibly marine-rich reefs. But venture a short way inland and you'll be enveloped in jungles where jaguars, ocelots and baboons roam, exotic birdlife is prolific, and isolated jungle lodges provide a base for some truly inspiring hiking. Adventurers can try zip-lining, caving, waterfall-rappelling and river-canoeing within an hour's drive of Belize City. The ancient Maya ruins and the Maya people themselves are further highlights – cacao farms and homestays in the Maya villages of the Deep South provide a new means of immersing yourself in the local culture.

UNMISSABLE EXPERIENCES

• The defining image of Belize is the Blue Hole Natural Monument, a dramatic 124m-deep sinkhole where sheer walls plunge to create a diving adrenaline rush. The adjacent Lighthouse Reef atoll also offers astonishing underwater wildlife.

• Belize's most famous subterranean adventure is Actun Tunichil Muknal (ATM Cave) – the Cave of the Stone Sepulchre. A guided tour takes you deep into the ancient Maya underworld in search of the 'Crystal Maiden'.

• It's difficult to say which is the best of the well-preserved Maya sites scattered around Belize. Altun Ha is the most accessible from the cayes, Caracol the most remote, Lamanai the most comprehensive and Xunantunich among the most impressive. Take your pick.

TIME YOUR VISIT

The dry (high) season is from January to April. Monsoon rains, occasional hurricanes and high humidity keep visitor numbers down from May to November. Whale-shark season is March to June, while scarlet macaws gather in the village of Red Bank from January to March. The biggest annual festivities are the September Celebrations.

• By Paul Harding

TOP 10
REGIONS

Piedmont, Italy / The Catskills, USA / Northern Peru
The Red Centre, Australia / Scotland's Highlands and islands
Russian Far East / Gujarat, India / Manitoba, Canada
Normandy, France / Elqui Valley, Chile

The elegant
city centre
of Turin,
Piedmont's
urban core

01

TOP 10 REGIONS

PIEDMONT, ITALY

██████ This landlocked northwestern corner of Italy – former Savoy stronghold, crucible of Italian nationhood and 20th-century industrial powerhouse – is adept at playing to its strengths but not always so good at selling its considerable charms to visitors. However, with Turin's contemporary-arts and electronic-music scenes flourishing, a very special self-portrait of Leonardo da Vinci squirrelled away in the city's Biblioteca Reale, sublimely remote Alpine walking trails *and* a clutch of exquisitely bucolic villages and valleys offering up arguably Italy's best reds (wine) and whites (truffles), it might not be just the savvy, arty, foodie traveller's secret for much longer.

Population: 4.5 million
Main town: Turin
Languages: Italian (official), Piedmontese, Occitan, Franco-Provençal, Insubric, Walser (spoken)
Unit of currency: Euro
How to get there: Turin is serviced by a handful of international flights. Milan's Malpensa is two hours away by road and there are regular fast trains from Milan to Turin, as well as direct services to Paris or Nice that take about five hours.

TELL ME MORE...

Turin's impressive cultural assets dot the elegant Savoy city centre but it's in the capital's once-bleak industrial outskirts where you'll find new arts hubs such as the sprawling OGR and the Museo Ettore Fico. Italy's best nightlife also lies beyond the baroque piazzas and palazzi, with live venues and clubs clustered in Dora and San Salvario. And although the traditions of the Piedmontese table will definitely delight, Turin's explosive culinary and wine scene is now as much about bold innovation as it is providence and seasonality.

Still, rural Piedmont takes *slowness* very seriously – it's home to the Slow Food movement after all, including the university in

'Turin is a humble workshop town, but in the past 15 years we've rediscovered ourselves through art, music and food. Torino Contemporary Art Week, Today's Festival or my beloved Ristorante Consorzio are all about being brave enough to push boundaries.'
Gianluca Cannizzo, creative director, Laboratorio Zanzara and My Poster Sucks, Turin

ITINERARY
Four days in Piedmont

• In **Turin**, sip an espresso at tiny, boiserie-lined Al Bicerin, then explore the extraordinary, absorbing Egyptian artefacts on display at the city's Museo Egizio.

• Head out to **Castello di Rivoli** for one of Italy's best collections of Arte Povera works, then don 'Turin black' attire for a luxe aperitivo at historic Bar Cavour and a night in clubland.

• Head to **Barbaresco** to taste its namesake wine and nibble hazelnuts and Tome cheese at Le Rocche dei Barbari. A member of the winemaker's family will talk you through the sky under which each vintage grew – and the various soils below that.

• Stock up on chocolates in small but stately **Cuneo** before striking out to ski or hike the **Maritime Alps**.

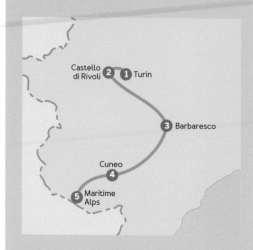

Bra dedicated to the subject – and the areas of Langhe, Roero and Monferrato produce some of the world's most sought-after (and stratospherically expensive) red wines, while managing to retain a dreamy, agrarian grace. To the west and the north there's epic hiking or low-key skiing in the Maritime Alps, a dark and vertiginous collection of peaks, valleys and lakes bumping up against France.

UNMISSABLE EXPERIENCES

• Take the lift to the top of Turin's Mole Antonelliana to enjoy staggering views across the rooftops of this overwhelmingly flat city, with pretty Po-side hills on one side and a majestic curtain of Alpine peaks on the other. Back on ground level, take time to explore the cinema museum housed inside.

• Snag a table at Alba's La Piola during the Fiera Tartufo Bianco, where your truffle lust is only limited by your budget: a rasp- and scales-wielding waiter will happily keep shaving the fragrant nugget on your buttery *tajarin* (angel hair pasta) until you shout *'basta!'* and then tally up the cost.

TIME YOUR VISIT

Piedmont's appeal transcends the seasonal, and although you'll need to book accommodation well ahead during Alba's truffle festival in October and November, or in Alpine resorts over January, you can definitely snag bargains over most of the year and especially in summer when locals head to the coast.

• By Donna Wheeler

The hilltop town of La Morra and its vineyards

© MATT MUNRO / LONELY PLANET

Looking up into the
dome of Turin's
Basilica di Superga

THE CATSKILLS, USA

Fifty years ago in the heart of the Catskills, the Woodstock Festival became one of the watershed events that defined a generation. Although the flower children may now have grandkids of their own, the free-spirited ethos lives on in the indie-loving towns of this picturesque region in upstate New York. In recent years there's been an influx of creative farm-to-table restaurants, bespoke breweries and distilleries, and a growing array of arts collectives and high-profile concert venues. Speaking of concerts, August 2019 is the time to visit if you want to be a part of history – revelry and music will once again be in the air for the 50th anniversary of Woodstock.

The road slices
through Minnewaska
State Park Preserve

Population: 348,698
Main town: Woodstock
Language: English
Unit of currency: US dollar
How to get there: Three major airports serving NYC (JFK, LaGuardia and Newark) are within a few hours' drive. It's best to hire a car to get around, although Trailways buses serve some Catskills destinations (from NYC's Port Authority Bus Terminal).

TELL ME MORE...

Though it's just a few hours north of Manhattan, the lush peaks and forested valleys of the Catskills feel like a world removed from the bustle of New York City. Planted among the greenery, pretty towns such as Woodstock and Saugerties have photogenic main streets sprinkled with antique shops, vintage cafes and eco-minded eateries, all fine places to rub elbows with the artists, writers and other creative types who've fled the city for this peaceful enclave. The real draw, though, is the great outdoors. Climb to the top of a granite overlook and take in the seemingly endless expanse of rolling green hills, and you'll see why so many people have fallen under the spell of the Catskills. There are refreshing waterfalls to frolic beneath and lazy rivers to paddle down with bald eagles sometimes spotted overhead. The region also packs plenty of surprises, from astonishing sculpture gardens hidden in the forest to old-fashioned single-screen cinemas that seem straight out of the 1950s.

UNMISSABLE EXPERIENCES

• Get a taste of the Catskills' wild beauty on a 3km (round-trip) hike to Kaaterskill Falls. The

Boutiques in the hip Catskills town of Saugerties

two-stage waterfalls are among the highest in the eastern US, cascading some 80m down thick forested slopes.

• At the stunning Olana State Historic Site, you can visit a castle overlooking a scenic stretch of the Hudson River and the Catskills beyond. This 100-hectare estate was the grand vision of the famed 19th-century landscape painter Frederic Church, who incorporated traditional Victorian architecture with Middle Eastern decorative motifs. The result is a wild medley of wood, coloured brick, ceramic tile and stencilling, boasting surprising design elements (and artwork) throughout.

'If you're like me, you may never want to leave the Catskills. You may find yourself drawn to the independent spirit of its people and the serene beauty of its landscapes.'

Garret Jackson, musician and Ulster County resident

• **TIME YOUR VISIT**

A splendid four-season destination, the Catskills offers powdery downhill skiing in the winter, blooming wildflower-filled hikes in springtime, blazing fall foliage in autumn and outdoor festivals in the summer. If you missed the last big event, make your plans now to hit the 50th anniversary of Woodstock festivities in Bethel Woods this August, including performances by musicians who played at the original festival in 1969.

• By Regis St Louis

ITINERARY
Two to three days in the Catskills

• Enjoy the picturesque view over the Hudson from the lovely **Saugerties Lighthouse**, an 1869 landmark that also hosts an atmospheric B&B (reserve well ahead).

• Head to the heights of **Hunter Mountain** for skiing in the winter, zip-line canopy tours in the summer, and festivals throughout the year, including a four-day Mountain Jam fest in June.

• Stroll the colourful streets of **Woodstock**, checking out art galleries, eco-friendly boutiques and farm-to-table restaurants.

• Take in an outdoor concert and learn about the historic Woodstock Festival at the **Bethel Woods Center for the Arts**.

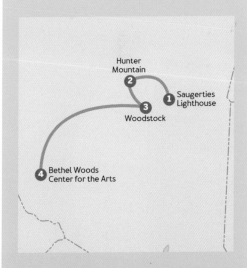

The crystal lakes of
Llanganuco Valley are
flanked by the Andes

03

03
BEST IN TRAVEL
2019

NORTHERN PERU

Northern Peru is a collection of superlatives, home to some of the oldest cultures on the continent and some of the wildest landscapes in the world. This region is an impressive distillation of what makes South American travel spectacular. In their dash to the south, many travellers bypass the great north. But as Machu Picchu has begun to reach tourist capacity, authorities have been implementing more travel infrastructure in the north – a cable car is now running at Kuélap to make the citadel more accessible, and the number of flights from Lima to the north has been increased, making 2019 the perfect time to visit this unjustly under-explored region.

© MAKASANA / GETTY IMAGES

71

Population: Approximately 9 million

Main towns: Huaraz, Trujillo, Cajamarca, Tarapoto, Chiclayo, Iquitos

Languages: Spanish and Quechua (official), Asháninka and a number of Amazonian languages (spoken)

Unit of currency: Peruvian sol

How to get there: Peru has numerous air connections to other cities in the Americas as well as Europe, with Lima serving as its primary hub. To access the north, visitors have a variety of options: catch a bus or flight to Huaraz to hike the Cordilleras, to Cajamarca to explore the northern highlands, or to Trujillo to swing along the north coast. The Amazon Basin has several access towns connected by river, water and air.

TELL ME MORE...

Northern Peru covers a wide expanse of land – as well as a number of juxtaposing ecosystems – from the swell-spotted coastline to the entrancing cloud forests of Chachapoyas, and the skyscraping peaks of the Cordilleras to the steamy Amazon rainforests.

Not only does the north offer staggering natural beauty, but for thousands of years it has been home to an array of diverse settlements, sprawling empires and remote villages, each leaving an imprint on this part of Peru and the people living here. Historic ruins pepper the region, ranging in size from the small anonymous huts in Parque Nacional Huascarán

'Drive from the desert in Chiclayo up to the Andes of Chachapoyas and down to the Amazon in Tarapoto. I can't imagine any other route so rich in landscapes, ecosystems, biodiversity and archaeology.'
Lluis Dalmau, hotel and ecotourism entrepreneur

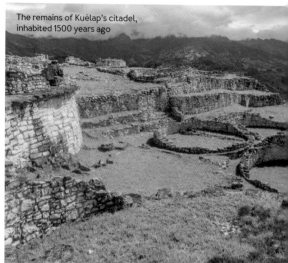
The remains of Kuélap's citadel, inhabited 1500 years ago

Spanish colonial architecture, Trujillo

03
BEST IN
TRAVEL
2o19

ITINERARY
Four weeks in northern Peru

- Take a quick flight from **Lima** to Huaraz to access the magnificent **Cordillera Blanca**. Parque Nacional Huascarán is home to more than 600 glaciers and close to 300 lakes.

- Catch a bus to colonial Trujillo, where you can walk among the ruins at **Chan Chan**, the largest pre-Columbian city in the Americas and the biggest adobe city in the world.

- From Chachapoyas, organise an excursion to monumental **Kuélap**, a spectacular citadel that rivals Machu Picchu's grandeur but lacks the crowds.

- Head east to Tarapoto and fly to **Iquitos**, the world's largest city that can't be reached by road. This surprisingly happening town is nestled in the dense Peruvian Amazon and serves as an ideal access point for river excursions.

to the monumental citadel of Kuélap. Though history looms large, this part of Peru hasn't been left in the past: cities such as Trujillo, Cajamarca, Huaraz and Mánorca hum with activity and are good places to hobnob with travellers and locals alike.

UNMISSABLE EXPERIENCES

- Climb through a series of grassy valleys, rocky inclines and high-altitude plateaux to reach serene Laguna 69, a celestial blue glacial lake in the heart of the Cordillera Blanca. The hike is tough but you'll hardly notice thanks to the intoxicating panorama of icy mountain giants, purple wildflowers and friendly Peruvian cows.

- Grab your board and hop along the north's coastal towns for the ultimate Peruvian surf tour. Destinations such as Huanchaco – with its reed fishing boats – resort-chic Máncora, and laidback Playa Lobitos each offer a unique twist on the surfing experience. And if you find yourself feeling a bit waterlogged, there are many pre-Columbian ruins to explore nearby.

TIME YOUR VISIT

Though Peru has several different weather patterns, June to August is the dry season in the highlands and rainforest, and the best time to hit the trail. The coast's high season actually contrasts with the rest of the country's rainy season (December to February), so head west to find a sandy respite from the soggy interior.

- By Bailey Freeman

THE RED CENTRE, AUSTRALIA

At the spiritual heart of Australia's Red Centre is the country's most recognised natural wonder, Uluru. In 2019 this sacred site is finally closing to climbers, almost 150 years after explorers decided to 'conquer the rock'. Instead, visitors will find that this World Heritage site – recognised for its outstanding natural and cultural values – conquers them. Learn about the unique world view of the traditional custodians of this place, and see the stars and the desert with new eyes. Explore Uluru-Kata Tjuta (Ayers Rock and the Olgas), Watarrka National Park (Kings Canyon) and Alice Springs nearby.

04

The iconic sight of Uluru at sunrise

Population: Approximately 30,000

Main town: Alice Springs

Languages: English, multiple Aboriginal languages (Arrernte, Warlpiri, Yankunytjatjara, Pitjantjatjara, Pintupi-Luritja, Ngaatjatjarra, Ngaanyatjarra, Alyawarr and Anmatyerr)

Unit of currency: Australian dollar

How to get there: You can fly to the Red Centre via Alice Springs or Ayers Rock airports from major Australian cities. It's a three-day drive from Sydney or Melbourne, or a two-day train trip from Adelaide or Darwin on *The Ghan*.

TELL ME MORE...

For visitors there are myriad ways to encounter indigenous Australia in the Red Centre, the non-official name given for the Northern Territory's rusty red southern desert region. Ayers Rock Resort (a name preferred by the local Anangu community) at Yulara, near Uluru-Kata Tjuta National Park, offers guided walks, Aboriginal astronomy tours and bush-tucker lessons, to name a few. The gastronomy here is infused with indigenous ingredients, from the high-end dining under the stars at Tali Wiru to the do-it-yourself barbecues with emu, kangaroo or barramundi.

For adventurers, the Red Centre can be explored on challenging hikes (the 223km Larapinta Trail is one of Australia's newest long-distance walks), helicopter flights, ballooning, mountain biking at Alice Springs, or camel touring. If you prefer a more leisurely travel experience, there are kitchen garden talks, nature walks, Segway tours and cycling around Uluru.

A black-footed rock wallaby in West MacDonnell National Park

© KERRY WHITWORTH / GETTY IMAGES

> '**Some who travel to Alice report a sense of belonging; many stay. There's a thriving community of creative people and amazing Aboriginal art from all the surrounding communities.**'
> *Kathleen, owner of Kathleen Buzzacott Art Studio*

UNMISSABLE EXPERIENCES

• Watch the sun rise and illuminate the massive sandstone monolith of Uluru, then take a guided walk at its base where you'll explore the pockmarked rock up close; hear Dreaming stories of *tjukurpa* (Aboriginal law, religion and custom, pronounced 'chook-orr-pa' in English); and see millennia-old rock art.

• Discover the history of European colonisers and the Afghan cameleers who explored this vast interior at Alice Springs Telegraph Station and Hermannsburg, famous as the one-time home of celebrated Aboriginal artist Albert Namatjira.

• On meandering bushwalks take in the colossal landscapes where white ghost gums contrast with crimson rocks and azure skies. Or embark on an early-morning bike ride to have the epic terrain to yourself.

TIME YOUR VISIT

May to September is best for festivals – and cooler weather. From October 2019 visitors will no longer be allowed to 'climb the rock'. Summer months (November to February) are blazing hot, so extra sun-smart precautions must be taken.

• By Tasmin Waby

ITINERARY
One week in the Red Centre

• Soak up the local culture in **Alice Springs**: quirky cafes, art galleries and events such as the Henley-on-Todd Regatta, the Camel Cup and the Beanie Festival.

• Spot black-footed rock wallabies at the waterhole at **Simpsons Gap** in the West MacDonnell Ranges just outside town.

• Head to **Watarrka National Park** (Kings Canyon) for iconic views of the sheer 100m-high red canyon cliffs, either in a 4WD via Larapinta Drive or on luxuriously sealed highways.

• Pilgrimage to **Uluru-Kata Tjuta National Park** to see the iconic rock and visit *Field of Light*, the stunning desert installation by British artist Bruce Munro.

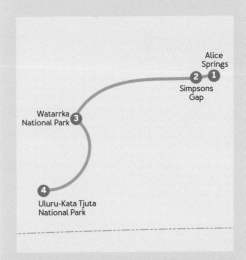

Alice Springs

2 **1**

Simpsons Gap

Watarrka National Park **3**

4

Uluru-Kata Tjuta National Park

Watching out for
'roos is a rule
of the road in
the Red Centre

05

The sea stacks at
Mangersta puncture
the Lewis coast

SCOTLAND'S HIGHLANDS AND ISLANDS

Whisky is the essence of the Highlands and islands, a thousand years of history and culture distilled. And whisky is experiencing a boom not seen since the 1890s: no fewer than 20 new distilleries opened in Scotland in the past two years, and at least 20 more will open by 2020. The distillery experience – learning about terroir, technique and tasting – is a great introduction to one of the wildest, least inhabited and most scenic parts of Europe. And its innovative and fast-developing accommodation sector, from purpose-built campervan parking spots to designer cottages modelled on ancient buildings, makes visiting remote areas easier than ever.

Population: 450,000

Main town: Inverness

Languages: English, Scottish Gaelic

Unit of currency: Pound sterling

How to get there: There are direct flights from London, Belfast, Bristol and Amsterdam to Inverness, and from Inverness to the Outer Hebrides. Alternatively, there are overnight sleeper trains from London to Inverness.

TELL ME MORE...

West Harris in the Outer Hebrides epitomises developments in the region, with gorgeous self-catering accommodation that includes a three-storey dry-stone replica of an Iron Age broch (defensive tower), a stunning modern art gallery and restaurant at Talla na Mara, and a suite of new campervan pitches. All are close to the famous white-sand beaches and turquoise waters of Luskentyre and Scarista, the Isle of Harris distillery, and the recently opened Hebridean Way hiking and biking trail.

The hugely successful North Coast 500 driving route has drawn crowds to the scenic glories of Assynt, Coigach and Torridon. But quieter roads beckon on the newly opened

Glenfinnan viaduct had a starring role in Harry Potter

© MIROSLAV_1 / GETTY IMAGES

Scotch and a sporran – a quintessential Highland pairing

© GEORGE CLERK / GETTY IMAGES

'**Where else could you be surfing on the coast in the morning and be snowboarding in the mountains by the afternoon. The region has a rich history, a stunning natural landscape and enviable local food and drink.'**

Gail Cleaver, general manager, the Macallan Visitor Experience

ITINERARY
Ten days in the Highlands and islands

• Eat out in the Highland capital **Inverness**, and day-trip to Culloden, scene of Bonnie Prince Charlie's final defeat, and the newly expanded visitor experience at the Macallan distillery.

• Go monster-hunting on **Loch Ness**, and continue along the Great Glen and the Road to the Isles, pausing at **Glenfinnan**'s railway viaduct (made famous in the Harry Potter films), to catch a ferry from Mallaig to **Lochboisdale**.

• Spend at least three days exploring the islands of the Outer Hebrides, taking in the white-sand beaches of **Harris** and the prehistoric standing stones at Callanish on **Lewis**.

• Catch another ferry from Stornoway to Ullapool, then wind your way through the magnificent mountain scenery of **Torridon** on your way back to Inverness.

North East 250, which links the Cairngorm mountains and Royal Deeside to the sea cliffs, beaches and fishing villages of Moray and Aberdeenshire, and the Snow Roads, a rollercoaster of a route that runs from Blairgowrie to Grantown-on-Spey over the two highest public highways in the UK.

UNMISSABLE EXPERIENCES
• Climb a mountain. The footpath up the iconic peak of Suilven has been repaired and upgraded in anticipation of increased popularity following the release of the 2017 movie *Edie*, in which it plays a starring role.

• Savour the region's sought-after seafood at one of the Highlands and islands' many fine restaurants. Go full linen and silverware at old stalwarts such as the Kylesku Hotel, or eat with your fingers at local favourites like Skye's Oyster Shed or Lewis's Scallop Shack

• Join a nature-watching trip and discover the wealth of wildlife that abounds here, from red deer, golden eagles and otters to whales, dolphins and basking sharks.

TIME YOUR VISIT
May and June are easily the best months, not just for good weather but to catch the blaze of wildflowers on the coastal machair (grass-covered sand dunes) and patches of snow lingering on the higher peaks. You'll also avoid the worst of the midges (small biting insects), which thrive in July and August becoming the curse of hikers and campers.

• By Neil Wilson

RUSSIAN FAR EAST

▬▬▬ **Russia's remotest corner** has undergone an impressive transformation in recent years, from overlooked backwater to regional lynchpin as Russia firmly turns its attentions towards its Asian neighbours. This new dynamism is most clearly seen in the elevation of its biggest city, Vladivostok, from regional capital to cultural and culinary stalwart. Both the Hermitage and the Mariinsky Theatre have opened important new spaces in the city in recent years, alongside home-grown big-hitters such as the Fabrika Zarya arts complex; there's little doubt that Vladivostok's star is in the ascendant. Elsewhere, the region's pristine nature and dramatic volcanoes are all more accessible than ever.

© SAIKO3P / SHUTTERSTOCK

06

Vladivostok's
cable-stayed
Zolotoy Bridge
opened to traffic
in 2012

'Take in Vladivostok's superb eating and drinking options in GUM Courtyard, have cocktails at Old Fashioned or Moonshine and party in the summer months with the cool kids at RA on the seafront.'

Alexei Sheyn, event planner, Vladivostok

Transfiguration Cathedral in Khabarovsk

© SHUTTERSTOCK / KONSTANTIN BAIDIN

Population: 6.3 million

Main town: Vladivostok

Language: Russian

Unit of currency: Russian rouble

How to get there: All major cities in the region have direct connections to Moscow, which is the gateway to the Russian Far East from Europe. Vladivostok, Khabarovsk, Petropavlovsk-Kamchatsky and Yuzhno-Sakhalinsk also have direct connections to Běijīng and Tokyo.

TELL ME MORE...

In the Russian Far East you're beyond even Siberia, so forget your idea of traditional travel destinations and head somewhere that even Russians consider a little 'out there'. Kamchatka – where the Ring of Fire has torn active volcanoes and geysers, hot springs and lava flow out of the landscape – is always going to be at the top of any adventurer's bucket list. It doesn't disappoint, due to dozens of exciting helicopter excursions, including a visit to Tolbachik volcano, where the rocks are still hot to the touch after its 2013 eruption.

Elsewhere in the vast region, a couple of recently established nature reserves offer a chance to see the endangered Amur tigers. You can also visit the ruins of the Gulag camp system in Magadan or experience life in the far north in remote Yakutsk, which is an unusual diamond-mining boomtown built on stilts over the permafrost.

UNMISSABLE EXPERIENCES

• Take one of the most exciting day trips imaginable and travel by helicopter deep into the smoking Valley of the Geysers, a unique and alien landscape unlike almost anywhere on Earth.

• The BAM railway, a little-known branch line

Departing Komsomolsk-na-Amure on the 3140km BAM railway

© PHILIP LEE HARVEY / LONELY PLANET

of the Trans-Siberian, is a feat of engineering that pushes a single train line through thousands of kilometres of wild Far Eastern taiga. It was a propaganda triumph for Stalin that is still celebrated by locals today.

• Voyage up the mighty Lena River to see the incredible 80km-long series of rock formations, the Lena Pillars. The magnificent 35-million-year-old geological features can be visited on a two-day cruise from Yakutsk.

TIME YOUR VISIT

In general, the summer months are the most comfortable and enjoyable for visiting the Russian Far East. Indeed, much of Kamchatka is only accessible in the short summer between late June and late August – this is when helicopter tours to the major volcanoes are possible. Winter is freezing but beautiful.

• By Tom Masters

ITINERARY
Two weeks in the Russian Far East

• Start in **Vladivostok**, the Far East's most vibrant and culturally interesting city, and enjoy superb museums, an exciting arts scene and stellar dining options.

• Jump aboard the Trans-Siberian railway to **Khabarovsk**, a real charmer of a city with a green riverside location and impressive tsarist architecture.

• Fly to **Yakutsk**, a city built on permafrost, where you can visit ice caves, get to know the Yakut culture and really experience life in the far north.

• End in **Kamchatka**, where you can take several incredible day trips to active volcanoes and do some excellent hiking amid spectacular natural surroundings.

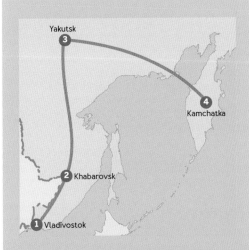

Yakutsk
3
Kamchatka
4
Khabarovsk
2
Vladivostok
1

Klyuchevskaya Sopka
in Kamchatka is one
of the world's highest
active volcanoes

07

The intricate sculptures of Rani-Ki-Vav stepwell in Patan

TOP 10 REGIONS

GUJARAT, INDIA

Wednesday 2 October 2019 is going to be a big day to be in Gujarat. Indian prime minister and Gujarat native, Narendra Modi, has budgeted 150 crore rupees (US$23m) to celebrate the 150th anniversary of the birth of Mahatma Gandhi, Gujarat's best known and most beloved son. But even amid all the fanfare there'll be room to breathe in Gujarat's calm and quiet corners: backwater townships with skies full of kites; lions, wolves, hyenas and wild asses wandering through serene nature reserves; and tribal communities painting arid Kachchh in rainbow colours with their mirrored and embroidered costumes.

Population: 63.8 million
Main town: Gandhinagar
Languages: Gujarati, Hindi
Unit of currency: Indian rupee
How to get there: Sardar Vallabhbhai Patel
International Airport is the gateway to Gujarat and is
handy for both historic Ahmedabad and its modern
neighbour, Gandhinagar. Trains run to cities across the
state from neighbouring Rajasthan, Madhya Pradesh
and Maharashtra.

TELL ME MORE

When Mohandas (Mahatma) Gandhi was born
in the sleepy town of Porbandar in 1869, the
Raj was running full throttle and Gujarat was
filling the coffers of the British Empire as the
'Manchester of the East'. One tumultuous
lifetime later, and the British were out on their
ears, the nation had its freedom and Gujarat
was incised into the national consciousness as
the birthplace of Indian independence.

　　In the 150th anniversary year of Gandhi's
birth, set your sights on Ahmedabad, where
the 'Great Soul' founded his ashram beside the
Sabarmati river and embarked on the Salt March
that proved to be the tiny acorn from which the
mighty oak tree of Indian independence grew.
Gandhi's Sabarmati Ashram is the focus of the
anniversary celebrations but the excitement
will spill over to Gandhi's birthplace in
Porbandar and his family home in Rajkot.

UNMISSABLE EXPERIENCES

• Walk in the footsteps of history in
Ahmedabad, from the medieval mosques
and mausoleums left behind by the Gujarat
sultanate to the Sabarmati Ashram, where
Gandhi lived almost without possessions,

ITINERARY
Eight days in Gujarat

• Kick off the Gujarati odyssey in **Ahmedabad**,
enjoying its museums, mosques and
mausoleums, and pausing to sup on delectable
Gujarati street food in the alleyways of
Bhatiyar Gali.

• Visit Gandhi's humble living quarters at
Sabarmati Ashram.

• Take the bus north to **Patan**, to feast your eyes
on the architectural wonder that is the Rani-ki-
Vav stepwell.

• Travel on to the **Wild Ass Sanctuary** in the
desolate Little Rann of Kachchh.

• Ride the rails south to spot Asiatic lions in **Gir
National Park**, before finishing up in the historic
Portuguese enclave of **Diu**.

Unesco-listed Rani-
ki-Vav was built in the
11th century

© LEONID ANDRONOV / GETTY IMAGES / ISTOCKPHOTO

formulating ideas to crumble an empire.

• Be humbled by the silence of Gir National Park, home to the last wild lions in Asia, or the Little Rann of Kachchh, where wolves, hyenas, antelopes and wild asses roam desolate salt plains.

• Encounter tribal culture in colourful Kachchh, where villagers cover everything that isn't nailed down with miniature mirrors and embroidery.

'I've lived in Gujarat for more than a decade, and I love it for its vibrancy and its friendly and peace-loving people.' *Jenu Devan, Managing Director, Gujarat Tourism*

TIME YOUR VISIT

The monsoon drenches Gujarat between June and September, bringing widespread flooding, even in desert areas. Visit after the rains have stopped for hot but not baking days and clear skies. Gandhi's birthdate, 2 October, is the focal point of celebrations in Ahmedabad and other towns associated with Gandhiji, coinciding with the start of the drier winter season.

• By Joe Bindloss

MANITOBA, CANADA

████ **Manitoba is, quite literally, at the centre of everything.** It's the geographical middle of Canada and a crucial point of encounter; the ancient Aboriginal people would trade their wares at what is now Winnipeg's downtown core. The capital city has retained its multicultural flavour, with over a quarter of its population having recently immigrated from nations as varied as the Philippines, Nigeria and India. Further north, near the township of Churchill, the province acts as an important crossroads for the country's megafauna – wandering bears and exploring whales. Increased air transfers and enhanced safari packages will now get travellers closer to nature than ever before.

A polar bear negotiates the ice of the Hudson Bay coast in Manitoba

08

Population: 1.3 million
Main town: Winnipeg
Languages: English
Unit of currency: Canadian dollar
How to get there: The Winnipeg James Armstrong Richardson International Airport is Manitoba's aviation hub, directly connecting the provincial capital to a variety of domestic and international destinations. By car, the closest major cities are in the United States: Minneapolis-St Paul (seven hours) in Minnesota, and Omaha, Nebraska (9½ hours). Winnipeg is also a stop on Canada's VIA Rail transnational train service between Toronto and Vancouver. Churchill is a two-hour flight from Winnipeg; the train to Churchill is a hotly debated topic as it's currently inoperable, though plans to reboot the service are underway.

TELL ME MORE...

On Saturday nights in Churchill, the locals gather at the Tundra Inn's ramshackle bar for a trivia match – six rounds of rousing questions covering everything from obscure weather phenomena to Justin Bieber lyrics. The competition is savage at first, dissolving into laughter as the beers go down the hatch. Anyone visiting town is invited to join in and witness the Manitoban spirit at its finest; a people fiercely proud of their homeland and unconditionally welcoming. The province has been the brunt of a joke or two – metropolitan Canucks often write off the region as a flyover swath of prairies – but Manitoba offers Canada's truest and most varied sense of the North. Uncountable blue lakelets promise abundant ice fishing and coveted cottage living, and when the tree line thins out, dazzling arctic wildflowers light the way

ITINERARY
One week in Manitoba

- Explore the surprising cosmopolitan flourishes of downtown **Winnipeg**, including the award-winning Canadian Museum for Human Rights, and the Forks National Historic Site, a meeting place of Aboriginal people for over 6000 years.
- Choose one of Manitoba's 100,000-plus inland lakes and drop in a line for some top-tier angling and ice fishing. Our pick is **Lake Winnipeg**, the province's largest, which feels like an inland sea.
- Fly to the northern outpost of **Churchill** to spy on roving polar bears from the safety of your safari cart.
- Hit the waters of the **Hudson Bay** to kayak with the thousands of white, slippery belugas that swim by each summer.

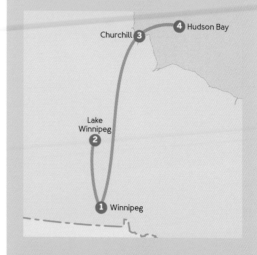

'My favourite thing about Manitoba is the sky – the cotton-candy clouds billow as they sail by; at night the aurora explodes with unimaginable colours.' *Rob Knaggs, expat, cellist and environmental activist.*

Experiencing the aurora borealis in Marchand

© DANIEL HUEBNER / SHUTTERSTOCK

towards the coast – the chilly, iceberg-ridden Hudson Bay, where polar bears paddle and belugas splash and spray.

UNMISSABLE EXPERIENCES

Churchill's colony of scavenging polar bears has long outnumbered the township's human population during its autumn months, which are the best time for viewing, but the most soul-stirring adventure in Manitoba's north takes place during the summer, when almost 60,000 beluga whales migrate through the warmer waters of the Hudson Bay to birth their young in the shallows. In July and August, take the opportunity to ply the gentle waves in a kayak, stand-up paddleboard or inflatable Zodiac raft,

and you may chance an encounter with these curious and highly communicative creatures. Armchair travellers can also get a glimpse of the whales thanks to explore.org's live underwater cameras.

TIME YOUR VISIT

There's no wrong time to visit Manitoba, it just depends on what you're hoping to see. Prime polar bear viewing occurs in October and November, while the belugas swim by during July and August. In winter (January to March) the fluorescent curtains of the aurora shine overhead. The wildflowers burst forth with their own kaleidoscopic palette in spring.

• By Brandon Presser

09

The island commune
and abbey of Mont
St-Michel

NORMANDY, FRANCE

Dotted with delightful beaches, Normandy's wild yet romantic coastal landscape is complemented by some of the tastiest seafood, creamiest cheeses and most lip-smacking ciders you can lay your hands on. History hounds won't know where to start in this heritage-rich region and 2019 is the year to stop by for the 75th anniversary of D-Day, so expect commemorative events and festivities galore. Additionally, the city of Rouen is getting ready for the arrival of ships from all over the world to sail up the River Seine during the 30th Rouen Armada, which is held once every four to six years and draws millions of spectators.

'Normandy is a stunning medley of differing landscapes – raw coastline, beautiful beaches, the ample, green countryside – and there's an immense gastronomic heritage to boot. Throw in some sun and it's perfect.'

Christèle and François Lecornu, owners of the Logis Les Remparts B&B, Bayeux

Population: 3.4 million

Main town: Rouen

Language: French

Unit of currency: Euro

How to get there: Normandy is accessible by train from Paris. Car ferries link Normandy ports with the UK and Ireland. Regional airports in Normandy include Rouen and Caen. Driving a car is the best way to get around.

Rouen's Rue du Gros-Horloge

TELL ME MORE...

You'll want to take time to savour the medieval good looks of Rouen, a gorgeous city on the River Seine that serves as a gateway to the region. Then get behind the wheel to soak up those Normandy shoreline sensations in low gear along the enticing Côte d'Albâtre (Alabaster Coast) and stop at breezy roadside viewpoints at will. A trail of fine seafood restaurants follows a dramatic coastline through a string of seaside towns and villages along the minor roads: Pourville-sur-Mer, Varengeville-sur-Mer, Veules-les-Roses and on to St-Valery-en-Caux, Veulettes-sur-Mer, Les Petites Dalles, Fécamp and one-of-a-kind Étretat. The solemn D-Day beaches and awe-inspiring cemeteries await beyond handsome

Honfleur and charming Caen, with the world-renowned Bayeux Tapestry on show in its namesake medieval town. The end of your journey leads you on to the cusp of Brittany, where the spectacle of Mont St-Michel forms one of the best photo ops in northern France.

UNMISSABLE EXPERIENCES

• Take time to fully understand the magnitude of how WWII afflicted Normandy at the gripping and haunting Le Mémorial – Un Musée pour la Paix in Caen. Give yourself at least half a day to do it justice.

• Time your arrival to watch the tides sweep around Mont St-Michel and grab a ringside view from the ramparts, followed by an exploration

ITINERARY
A week in Normandy

- Start with **Rouen**'s imposing Cathédrale Notre Dame, dominating the heart of town and most famously depicted by Impressionist painter Claude Monet in varying light conditions.
- Drive through the coastal villages of the Côte d'Albâtre from **Dieppe** to the beach at **Étretat** with its sublime cliffs and viewpoints: Falaise d'Aval and Falaise d'Amont.
- Stop by the charming town of **Bayeux** to admire the astonishing artistic complexity and brilliance of its celebrated tapestry.
- Nothing prepares you for the harrowing impact of the endless marble crosses at the **Normandy American Cemetery & Memorial**.
- Explore the narrow medieval lanes and alleys of picturesque **Mont St-Michel**.

of the magnificent Abbaye du Mont St-Michel crowning the island.

- Choose a sunny day to climb up to the remains of Richard the Lionheart's castle, Château Gaillard, above Les Andelys for sublime views of the Seine looping off into the distance.

TIME YOUR VISIT

Summer is the optimum season: for 2019, make it June when the 75th anniversary D-Day commemorations and Rouen Armada are underway. Avoid winter when it's cold and shutters are up at many hotels, sights and restaurants. Check the tide tables for the best days of the month to visit Mont St-Michel.

- By Damian Harper

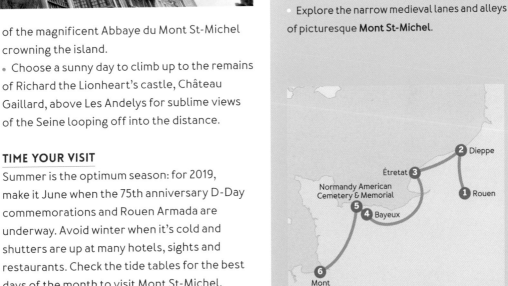

A view of the arch and chalk needle of Falaise d'Aval on Normandy's Côte d'Albâtre

ELQUI VALLEY, CHILE

Near the southern edge of the vast Atacama Desert, mountain rivers wind their way through vine-covered hillsides, chiselled peaks and serene villages slumbering beneath star-filled night skies. This is the Elqui Valley, one of northern Chile's most alluring regions. Though its charms are many — 320 days of sunshine, birthplace of a Nobel Prize–winning poet and epicentre of Chile's pisco production — the valley has remained largely hidden from the world's gaze. However, word is slowly getting out about this remarkable region and astrotourists are coming in increasing numbers to view its famously clear skies, particularly in 2019 when a total solar eclipse will pass directly overhead.

Witnessing daybreak over
Elqui Valley from Las
Campanas Observatory

10

The valley's verdant vineyards in spring

© KSENIA RAGOZINA | SHUTTERSTOCK

Population: 27,800
Main town: Vicuña
Language: Spanish
Unit of currency: Chilean peso
How to get there: The main gateway to the region is the town of Vicuña, 90 minutes' drive east of the city of La Serena, where you can catch (one-hour) flights to Santiago.

'Nothing compares to discovering the Elqui Valley by bike. Surrounded by green vineyards under the all-year-round blue sky, the setting is simply spectacular.'

Adeline Barré, co-founder of Elki Magic tours

TELL ME MORE...

Over the years, the Elqui Valley has acquired a reputation as a mystical centre, and some people are convinced that its hillsides have special properties. New Age seekers, psychics and swamis are drawn along its so-called *ruta de la sanación*, or 'healing path'. The valley's dark skies attract both ufologists and amateur astronomers. In fact, these are some of the clearest skies on the planet and at observatories scattered around the region you can enjoy guided night tours of celestial wonders.

Chile's first Nobel laureate, the poet Gabriela Mistral, grew up in the region and drew inspiration from its idyllic landscapes. Her life is commemorated in Vicuña, the town where she was born, and in Montegrande, where she attended primary school. Her burial site, on a nearby hillside, draws a handful of literary pilgrims. More visitors, however, come to the valley to taste its fiery piscos produced in vineyards that date back to the 19th century.

UNMISSABLE EXPERIENCES

• Learn about the wonders of the cosmos on a star-filled astronomy tour. Just outside Vicuña, small-scale operator Alfa Aldea gives astronomy tours led by convivial young scientists. You'll listen to the sounds in the heavens via radio telescope while enjoying a glass or two of Chilean wine, followed by open-air observation in the amphitheatre. Steaming cups of soup and blankets take the bite off the chill night air while astronomers guide you through the night sky with laser pointers. The evening culminates with a mesmerising look at planets, nebula and galaxies through high-spec telescopes.

TIME YOUR VISIT

Throughout the year, the Elqui Valley offers abundant sunshine and crisp nights. Many travellers skip Chile in the colder winter months (June to August), when some guesthouses and tour operators close. The exception will be in 2019, when the valley will be a magnificent place to watch the total solar eclipse on 2 July.

• By Regis St Louis

ITINERARY
Three to four days in the Elqui Valley

• Start in **Vicuña** and visit the Museo Gabriela Mistral, dedicated to Chile's first Nobel Prize–winning poet, in the pretty town that inspired her writing.

• Spend a night or two in the secluded valley of **Cochiguaz**, gateway to memorable hiking and horse riding in the region.

• Embark on guided treks by day and enjoy first-rate cooking by night in the tranquil village of **Pisco Elqui**.

• Sip your way through some of Chile's finest pisco on a tasting tour at the artisanal distillery of **Los Nichos**.

• Browse for locally made arts and crafts in the **Horcón** market set in the riverside village of the same name.

LONELY PLANET'S

TOP 10 CITIES

Copenhagen, Denmark / Shēnzhèn, China / Novi Sad, Serbia
Miami, USA / Kathmandu, Nepal / Mexico City, Mexico / Dakar, Senegal
Seattle, USA / Zadar, Croatia / Meknès, Morocco

01

Harbourside at Nyhavn in central Copenhagen

COPENHAGEN, DENMARK

Denmark's capital of cool is unstoppable. New-Nordic Noma has gourmands swooning with its new digs, urban farm and ground-breaking Scandinavian menus. The city's booming street-food scene is smashing it on Refshaleøen, where a former shipyard is now rebooted food and craft market Reffen. Amusement park Tivoli Gardens is beating the winter blues with a new February season, while waste-management centre Amager Bakke has jaws dropping with its rooftop ski slope and hiking trails. The Danish Architecture Centre has moved into Rem Koolhaas' buzz-inducing cultural centre BLOX, while the anticipated mid-2019 completion of the Cityringen metro line means even easier cross-town adventures.

Population: 1.9 million
Language: Danish
Unit of currency: Danish krone
How to get there: Copenhagen Airport is
Scandinavia's busiest air hub, with direct flights to
cities in Europe, North America and Asia. Efficient
metro and regional trains connect the airport to the
city centre.

TELL ME MORE...

Clean, green and compact, Copenhagen
is an enviable urban role model. Bicycles
outnumber cars in the inner city, while the
bracing, deep-blue harbour is clean enough
for a summertime dip. Copper towers and
turrets may still dominate the skyline, but
this is a city well versed in the cutting edge.
Cobbled streets boast sustainable menus,
trend-setting design and racks hung with
stylish, often boundary-pushing fashion.
Centuries-old palaces, churches and
warehouses share streets and waterways
with bold contemporary architecture, while
the city's former Meatpacking District hums
with galleries, locavore eateries and on-
point indie bars. Well-curated museums
burst with capital, from Viking bling and

'A morning bike ride through
Copenhagen in the springtime is
second to none. I cycle through
picturesque Søndermarken,
zigzagging through hip Vesterbro
and cycling along fashionable
Grønningen to the Citadel.'
Christian Struckmann Irgens, vice president
of Mystery Makers

ITINERARY
Three days in Copenhagen

- Snap the perfect Instagram shot along
colourful, boat-lined **Nyhavn** canal and take
a one-hour harbour cruise for a relaxing city
overview.
- Snoop around Christian IV's royal digs at
moated Renaissance castle **Rosenborg Slot.**
- Lose yourself on the atmospheric streets of
the **Latin Quarter,** home to Vor Frue Kirke and
its series of sculptures by eminent Danish artist
Bertel Thorvaldsen.
- Ponder French and Danish masterpieces at
eclectic art museum **Ny Carlsberg Glyptotek**.
- Eat, drink and party in Vesterbro's perennially
cool Meatpacking District, **Kødbyen.**
- Cycle along the Copenhagen Lakes to multi-
culti **Nørrebro,** the city's bohemian heartland.

Inside the new Noma

On the menu at Noma: stuffed
Queen clams from northern Norway

royal jewels to Danish industrial design and Scandinavia's largest collection of Islamic art. Many of these museums are within steps of lush, preened parks, themselves never short of picnicking locals on summer days. *Velkommen* to a European city living at its most enlightened.

UNMISSABLE EXPERIENCES

• Savour the region's terroir and ingenuity at one of Copenhagen's lauded New-Nordic restaurants. Top choices include Noma and Kadeau (book months in advance), as well as the more moderately priced Høst and Mes.
• Catch the train to Louisiana Art Museum, famed for its world-class collection of Danish and international modern art, its modernist architecture, sculpture garden and dreamy

setting amid magnificent trees by the Baltic Sea.
• Follow Hans Christian Andersen's lead and indulge your inner child with an evening at Tivoli Gardens. Shamelessly enchanting, Europe's oldest amusement park offers rides both tame and terrifying, concerts and fairy-tale city views.

TIME YOUR VISIT

April and May scintillate with post-winter energy and flowers, while June to August offer long days, a festive vibe and bigger crowds. September is often mild, while late September and October deliver vibrant autumn foliage. The gloom of November and December is countered by *gløgg* (mulled wine) and Tivoli's Christmas season.

• By Cristian Bonetto

The Copenhagen
cityscape – still
'wonderful, wonderful'

SHĒNZHÈN, CHINA

Welcome to China's most innovative city – Shēnzhèn – the 'Silicon Valley' of China. Drawn to its slew of new design openings and tech innovation, creatives are swarming to Shēnzhèn, just over the border from Hong Kong in mainland China. Previously known as a cheaper nightlife alternative to Hong Kong, Shēnzhèn now has a strumming indie-music scene, cool cafes, a small contingent of craft brewers and a whole new arts district risen from the remains of former warehouses. The past three years have seen the openings of Design Society, in conjunction with London's V&A museum, as well as the Museum of Contemporary Art & Planning Exhibition (MOCAPE) and heritage art village OCT Loft.

MOCAPE MUSEUM, SHENZHEN, COOP HIMMELB(L)AU ARCHITECTS, ©DUCCIO MALAGAMBA, BARCELONA

The Museum of
Contemporary Art &
Planning Exhibition
(MOCAPE) opened
in 2016

02

Population: 12.5 million
Languages: Mandarin, Cantonese
Unit of currency: Renminbi (yuàn)
How to get there: Shēnzhèn is served by Bǎo'ān
International Airport, with a growing list of flights to
international destinations. Railways link Shēnzhèn
with other parts of mainland China and Hong Kong's
MTR goes to the border, while ferries depart for Hong
Kong and Macau. The final section of the Běijīng–Hong
Kong high-speed rail line, connecting Shēnzhèn with
Kowloon West, opened in late 2018.

TELL ME MORE...

Shēnzhèn has grown from a tiny fishing village
into a 12-million-strong megalopolis in less
than three decades. Its line-up of technology
firms makes it the first port of call for China's
young tech graduates, lending the city a
youthful, creative and forward-thinking vibe.

At the end of 2017, Shēnzhèn converted
its 16,359 buses (more than the combined bus
fleets of North America's five largest cities) to
electric and it has invested ¥111.8 billion (US$17.8
billion) in sustainable development, including
plans to make all of its taxis electric-powered
by 2020.

The year 2019 will see Shēnzhèn connected
to neighbouring Hong Kong by a new high-
speed rail line, the final segment along the epic
2230km Běijīng–Hong Kong HSR route. The city
will also host the WTA Finals from 2019, pulling
in a new set of sporting fans.

Shēnzhèn's long-standing draws range
from the quirky to the delicious: a developing

Night falls on Shēnzhèn's
futuristic skyline

© YONGYUAN DAI / GETTY IMAGES

modern food scene, weird and wonderful theme parks, underground nightlife and Opium War–era historical sights.

'As a young immigrant city, Shēnzhèn is filled with youthfulness and energy. I thnk the best place to hang out is Coco Park. It is very centrally located and an area filled with great bars, cafes, restaurants and stores.'

Erica Zhuang, hospitality professional

UNMISSABLE EXPERIENCES

• Design Society, MOCAPE and OCT Loft will keep you occupied during the day. By night lay your head on a designer pillow in the minimalist-chic Muji Hotel.

• Window of the World is a quirky theme park where world landmarks are rendered in miniature, while Splendid China miniaturises China's most well-known sights.

• Shēnzhèn is a base for China's growing indie-music scene, with several festivals and regular shows at venues like B10 Live House, Brown Sugar Jar and Yīdùtáng. Sup some craft beer at taphouses of local breweries such as Bionic Brew, Peko Brewing Co and ET Brewery.

TIME YOUR VISIT

Shēnzhèn is best visited in winter, spring or autumn, when the weather is mild. Summers here can be hot, humid and rainy, and there is a risk of typhoons from July to September. Tennis fans should book ahead for the WTA Finals in October 2019.

• By Megan Eaves

ITINERARY
Five days in Shēnzhèn

• The sleek Fumihiko Maki–designed **Design Society** opened in 2017 in conjunction with the V&A in London, and features a rotating selection of design exhibitions, artist studios and landscaped gardens.

• Head to **Yīdùtáng** in OCT Loft and then wander up the road to the **B10 Live House** to check out what's new in China's indie-music scene.

• Designed by architects Coop Himmelb(l)au, **MOCAPE** is a gargantuan contemporary art gallery with a cloud-like mirrored atrium.

• Don't miss the bizarre theme park **Window of the World**, which portrays all of the world's landmarks in miniature, and grab a cold craft beer or three at nearby **Bionic Brew** afterwards.

03

Looking towards the
Name of Mary church
in Novi Sad

NOVI SAD, SERBIA

▬▬▬ **Elegant yet easygoing,** Novi Sad basks in the limelight, defying its second-city status and boldly living up to its moniker. Serbia's 'New Garden' hosts the rocking EXIT festival, whose 20th edition coincides with the city's stint as the 2019 European Youth Capital. Headlining this revival, the Petrovaradin Citadel's Lower Town is getting a facelift, and the dilapidated Chinatown has blossomed into an alternative-culture district. Bursting with creative energy, new Gradić Fest is reinvigorating Petrovaradin through music, film, theatre and art, as Novi Sad gears up to wear another crown – that of the 2021 European Capital of Culture.

Crowds at the city's renowned EXIT music festival

© ALEKSANDAR KAMASI / SHUTTERSTOCK

Population: 341,625
Languages: Serbian (official), Hungarian, Slovak and Rusyn also spoken
Unit of currency: Dinar
How to get there: The nearest airport is in Belgrade, which is well connected to major international destinations. Belgrade has hourly bus (one hour) and train (90 minutes) services to Novi Sad. The more adventurous can cycle into the city along the EuroVelo 6 route, or sail in style on a Danube river cruise from Budapest.

TELL ME MORE...

Radiating a youthful and multicultural vibe – thanks to its 80,000-strong student population and 20-plus nationalities – Novi Sad is graced with gorgeous Austro-Hungarian architecture, lending this outpost of the Balkans a typical Mitteleuropean feel. The capital of Vojvodina province is aptly dubbed 'the Serbian Athens':

its esteemed galleries, museums and theatres formed the cradle of national culture throughout the 18th and 19th centuries. Away from the old town's pastel-hued facades, the avant-garde clubs of gritty Chinatown have street cred in spades.

The formidable Petrovaradin Citadel may be famed as the 'State of EXIT', but there's more to this baroque jewel, including art ateliers and 16km of spooky subterranean labyrinths. A splendid stretch of sand just across the Danube, the Štrand beach is Novi Sad's summer playground. Time-honoured epicurean hangouts – salaši (farmsteads) and čarde (riverside inns) – dot the city surrounds; a short bus ride away, the bucolic Fruška Gora hills beckon with dozens of family wine cellars, hiking trails and monasteries to explore.

ITINERARY
Long weekend in Novi Sad

• Brave the maze of tunnels within the mighty **Petrovaradin Citadel** and soak up the views from its Clock Tower plateau.

• Delve into centuries of the region's history at the **Museum of Vojvodina,** where the prized possessions include three golden Roman helmets.

• Survey a treasure trove of Serbian art, from baroque to modernism, in the **Gallery of Matica Srpska.**

• Ramble around the **Chinatown** creative district, checking out the goings-on at alternative clubs Fabrika and The Quarter.

• Sample the local dessert drop *bermet* on a leisurely tour of the wineries scattered around **Fruška Gora National Park.**

UNMISSABLE EXPERIENCES

• The sandy Štrand beach and the green haven of Fisherman's Island are perfect spots to while away an afternoon. Pick up a two-wheeler from NS Bike to pedal along the Danube Cycling Path, or hit the water in a kayak or canoe with Dunavski Rafting. At sunset, join the carousing crowds on *splavovi* (floating nightclubs).

• For a veritable slow-food feast, traditional Vojvodinian taverns can't be beaten. Top choices include the romantic, riverside Čarda Aqua Doria, and the farmstead-style extravaganza of Lazin Salaš in the old town. The *riblji paprikaš* (fish stew), featuring freshly caught river bounty, is delicious.

'I love walking on Danube quay, enjoying magnificent sunset views of the Petrovaradin Fortress, and take my morning coffee at Špajz 123, a small restaurant with unique Vojvodinian spirit.' *Valentina Antić, International Cooperation Coordinator, European Youth Capital Novi Sad 2019*

TIME YOUR VISIT

Summer is the best time to visit. You can experience the EXIT revelry in July or Petrovaradin's Gradić Fest in early September, and go cycling or hiking in Fruška Gora. December's Winter Fest brings a fairy-tale atmosphere with a Christmas market and ice skating in Danube Park.

• By Brana Vladisavljevic

TOP 10 CITIES

MIAMI, USA

Famed for its beautiful beaches and buzzing nightlife, Miami has long captivated travellers seeking a slice of tropical paradise while the rest of North America shivers. Although the Magic City still makes a fine wintertime escape, the past few years have seen Miami transform into a burgeoning centre for the arts, a foodie destination and an innovator in urban design. Miami's downtown continues to be rejuvenated with the arrival of a celebrated $305-million science museum, while the Design District has become a cultural magnet with new eye-catching architecture (including the Museum Garage and the Institute of Contemporary Art), public art installations and expansive new cultural programming.

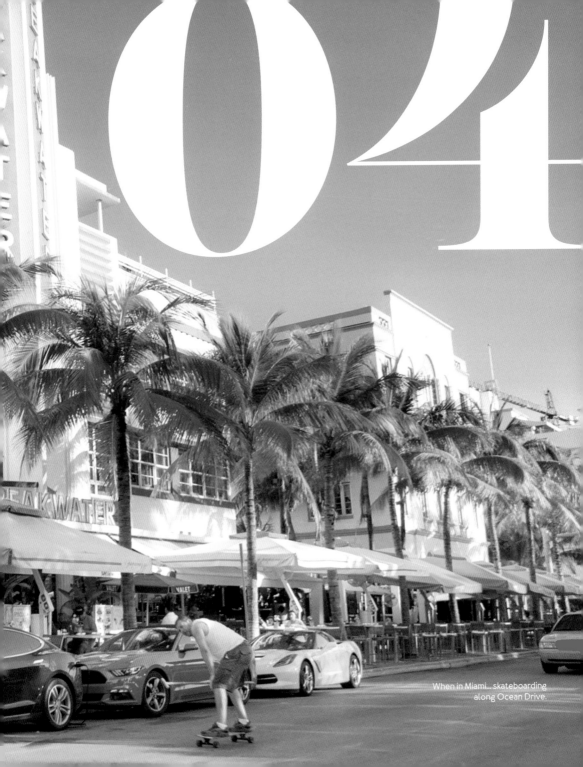

04

When in Miami... skateboarding
along Ocean Drive.

Population: 545,500

Languages: English, Spanish

Unit of currency: US dollar

How to get there: You'll find excellent international and domestic connections from Miami International Airport, which is located six miles northwest of downtown.

TELL ME MORE...

Art Basel Miami hosts top artists and gallerists from across the globe during its annual show, the biggest contemporary art event in America. Yet you needn't wait until December to experience Miami's artistic side. The ever-changing Wynwood Walls showcases the talents of some of the world's great street artists, and has reshaped the once-industrial 'hood into a dining and drinking destination, sprinkled with microbreweries, creative fusion eateries, and celebrated bakeries and coffee roasters, plus dozens of art galleries.

Further south, Miami's downtown has become a cultural destination in its own right. The brilliantly designed Pérez Art Museum Miami sits next to the brand-new 23,000-sq-metre Phillip & Patricia Frost Museum of Science, and just across the street from the Adrienne Arsht Center, one of Miami's premier performing arts venues. This is just the beginning of Miami's myriad attractions, from biologically rich tropical gardens to grand mansions built in the style of Renaissance chateaux.

UNMISSABLE EXPERIENCES

• Spend the day in steamy South Beach. Take a morning stroll along the golden sands, when the light is at its finest, then head inland

ITINERARY
Three to four days in Miami

• Get an eyeful of bold designs and pastel hues in the Art Deco Historic District. A good place to start is the **Art Deco Museum** right on photogenic Ocean Dr.

• Go art-gazing at the waterfront **Pérez Art Museum Miami,** home to some of Miami's best temporary exhibitions. Be sure to check out the sculpture garden and have a bite at the excellent on-site cafe.

• Check out the fantastical **Wynwood Walls,** a renowned collection of large-format street art in the indie-loving neighbourhood of Wynwood.

• Step into a fairy tale at the Renaissance-inspired mansion and the lushly landscaped estate of **Vizcaya Museum & Gardens.**

The Pérez Art Museum Miami building was
designed by architects Herzog & de Meuron

to Ocean Dr and Collins Ave for a wander
among an astonishing collection of art-deco
architecture.

• Around lunchtime, walk up to Lincoln Rd
for an al fresco lunch on the city's best-loved
promenade, followed by window-shopping at
Lincoln Rd's colourful boutiques and galleries.

• Before sunset head over to one of the grand

'Miami is a special place in the world;
the mixture of both traditional and
new world cuisine has transformed
the city to be one of the strongest
culinary forces in the country.'
Grace Della, founder of Miami Culinary Tours

deco hotels (like the Kimpton Surfcomber)
for poolside drinks and ocean views. Cap the
night with cocktails and dancing in the secret
backroom of Bodega (hidden behind a taco
stand, of course).

TIME YOUR VISIT

Miami is at its liveliest from December to March,
when jet-setters arrive for big events like Art
Basel and the Art Deco weekend. For fewer
crowds, lower prices and balmier temperatures
come in April or May. Avoid the steamy summer
months (June to September, which also partly
coincide with hurricane season).

• By Regis St Louis

KATHMANDU, NEPAL

In the aftermath of the 2015 earthquake, news reports from Kathmandu showed a city broken and in mourning, but today the narrative is all about reconstruction and rejuvenation. Sure, there's work to do restoring the magnificent monuments that crumbled during the disaster, but historic sites are being returned to their former glory, and moves to calm the city's infamous traffic, smog and noise have made Kathmandu more liveable than it has been in decades. There's even reliable electricity and wi-fi as bonus creature comforts in the atmospheric and maze-like alleyways of the old city.

©DET-ANAN / SHUTTERSTOCK

Population: 1 million
Language: Nepali
Unit of currency: Nepali rupee
How to get there: Most visitors arrive into Kathmandu's Tribhuvan International Airport, a short pre-paid taxi ride from the city centre. Buses and jeeps run regularly to cities around Nepal and the border crossings to Tibet and India.

'With its manic streetlife and its labyrinth of alleys leading from one square to another, and another, life in Kathmandu is nothing less than pure theatre.'

Abhi Shrestha, manager, Rural Heritage/Snow Cat Travel

TELL ME MORE...

Kathmandu was always the haven at the end of the overland trail – a place to kick back and unwind after days in rattletrap buses or weeks tramping along Nepal's mountain trails. But in 2015, this oasis was rocked by an earthquake that toppled monuments, killed thousands and sent a nation into crisis.

Today, Kathmandu's party spirit pumps again, and the cafes, bars and restaurants of Thamel throng with travellers from across the globe, munching everything from *momos* (Tibetan dumplings) to Korean barbecues, Israeli *shawarma* and authentic Thai curries.

Despite obvious evidence of the disaster – collapsed masonry, stacked timbers, buildings propped up by poles – the city is easier to enjoy than it has been in years, thanks to a reliable

Snow peaks rise above the rim of the Kathmandu Valley

electricity supply and the banning of cars (and motor horns) from the city centre. As Kathmandu gears up for the South Asia Games in March 2019, this is a great time to wander its meandering backstreets, visit temples and overload the senses with the sights, sounds and smells of a city revived.

UNMISSABLE EXPERIENCES

• Climb the monkey-crowded steps to magnificent Swayambhunath Stupa. From this lofty eyrie – shaken, but not diminished, by the disaster – you can gaze out across the city streets and marvel not at what was lost but at how much has survived.
• Wander Kathmandu's warren of backstreets and hidden *bahal* courtyards and you'll stumble across centuries-old statues and carvings that would be tucked away behind museum glass anywhere else in the world.
• Dip into backpacker district Thamel's global buffet, snacking on *momos* here, panini there, and wash it all down with a mango daiquiri, a full-bodied espresso, or a warm pot of *tongba* (Himalayan millet beer).

TIME YOUR VISIT

Kathmandu is at its best from October to May, but invest in a yak-wool or cashmere blanket for the chilly period from December to February. If you have any flexibility, time your trip to coincide with Indra Jatra or another fantastic Kathmandu festival. Savvy travellers avoid the rain-drenched monsoon from June to September.

• By Joe Bindloss

ITINERARY
Three days in Kathmandu

• Start off in **Durbar Sq**, where you'll see some of Nepal's finest temple architecture, and also piles of stones and timbers from collapsed monuments awaiting reconstruction.
• Jostle past monkeys to reach gilded **Swayambhunath Stupa**, with its painted Buddha eyes gazing serenely out across the Kathmandu Valley.
• Cross the city and join the crowds of Tibetan pilgrims circling the gleaming white dome of mighty **Bodhnath**, now lovingly restored after the earthquake.
• Move on to **Pashupatinath**, the Hindu heart of Kathmandu, where *sadhus* (holy men) chant mantras in timeless temples, and funeral fires flicker solemnly on the banks of the sacred Bagmati River.

The watchful eyes of
Buddha gaze out across
the Kathmandu Valley
from the gilded tower
atop Bodhnath Stupa

MEXICO CITY, MEXICO

The Mexican capital bears witness to centuries of architectural design and artistic movements. The pre-Hispanic buildings of the Mexica rise from the city's soft ground while colonial cathedrals stand fast and modern wonders such as the Museo Soumaya sparkle in the ever-present sun. For these reasons, and more still, Mexico City was named World Design Capital in 2018. CDMX (Ciudad de México) is the sixth city and the first in the Americas to hold the title. As the creative class rise, they embrace the influence of centuries-old traditions, proving that design is an effective tool for economic, social and cultural development.

© MARIA SWARD

06

Mexico City's
Palacio de Bellas
Artes sits next to
Alameda Central
park

Population: 8.85 million

Language: Spanish

Unit of currency: Mexican peso

How to get there: The Aeropuerto Internacional Benito Juárez has international flights on 20 airlines. You can fly direct from more than 30 cities in the US and Canada, half a dozen each in Europe, South America and Central America and the Caribbean, and from Tokyo. Seven different airlines connect the capital to about 50 cities within Mexico. A new airport, scheduled to open in 2020, will almost double capacity.

TELL ME MORE...

The complex history of Mexico City is tangible in the city's incredible art, architecture and cuisine. The artistic creations of the Mexica people fill the Templo Mayor and the fascinating Museo Nacional de Antropología. With an eye towards educating the masses, world-renowned muralists Diego Rivera, José Clemente and David Alfaro Siqueiros filled the national buildings with evocative images influenced by the bas-relief designs of the Aztecs.

The cuisine also reaches back and pushes forwards: from the *tostadas* in the market in Coyoacán to a private seven-course dinner at a secret chef's table in the city's hippest neighbourhood, you can taste traces of the past combined with modern innovations. Fashion designers fill boutiques with modern takes on Huichol embroidery, while artisan markets are packed with original works from all over Mexico.

UNMISSABLE EXPERIENCES

While the city boasts more than 150 museums and a plethora of art galleries and distinct architectural and historic sites, you can't miss

ITINERARY
Three days in Mexico City

• Head straight for the **Zócalo**, once the centre of the Aztec universe, and explore the pre-Hispanic ruins at Templo Mayor. Dip inside the cathedral before admiring Diego Rivera's murals at **Palacio Nacional**.

• Check out the **Museo Nacional de Antropología** and take a stroll through Chapultepec Park.

• Taste some tequila or mezcal and listen to mariachi music at **Plaza Garibaldi**.

• Wander around the fountains and leafy paths of Alameda Central and compare muralism styles in the **Palacio de Bellas Artes**.

• Make time for **Xochimilco** and spend an afternoon gliding along ancient canals on a *trajinera* (gondola).

'I love the city's museums. A guava roll from Café NiN and a stroll through Chapultepec park followed by an art exhibition at MUAC or JUMEX is the perfect morning.'

Sara Aroeste, Associate Scholar, Mexico Cultural Travel

leafy Coyoacán and the homes of Frida Kahlo and Diego Rivera. After wandering through the Museo Frida Kahlo, known as La Casa Azul, and learning about her challenging life and passionate art, you can head to Museo Casa Estudio Diego Rivera y Frida Kahlo and see another side of the talented duo. Wander the cobbled streets of this delightful neighbourhood, browse the artisanal crafts at San Angel's Bazar Sábado market and have dinner on the charming Jardín Centenario.

TIME YOUR VISIT

The weather in Mexico City is mild year-round, despite the high altitude. The rainy season from June to September rarely has more than a couple of hours of rain a day. The beginning of November marks Día de Muertos (Day of the Dead); CDMX hosts a giant spectacle of a parade on the last Saturday in October.

• By Sarah Stocking

Tacos al pastor: a Mexican delicacy

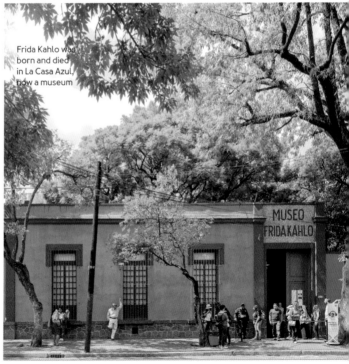

Frida Kahlo was born and died in La Casa Azul, now a museum

MUSEO FRIDA KAHLO

07

Dakar's delightful beach-lined shore

TOP 10 CITIES

DAKAR, SENEGAL

One of Africa's most dynamic cities, Dakar offers a dizzying mix of sun-kissed beaches, colourful markets and *mbalax*-fuelled nightclubs where snappily attired revellers emerge into the early-morning light as the first call to prayer drifts over the tropical landscape. Despite its myriad attractions, Senegal's seaside capital has long been overlooked by many travellers. All that is set to change as the city positions itself as a new travel hub in West Africa. Leading the way is the recent opening of a brand-new international airport, a US$600-million endeavour that's been more than 10 years in the making.

© DEREJE BELACHEW / 500PX

141

Population: 1.3 million

Languages: French, Wolof and 36 other African languages

Unit of currency: West African franc

How to get there: Dakar's new international airport, which opened in late 2017, has good connections to Europe. The airport is 50km southwest of the city centre.

TELL ME MORE...

The energy on the streets is palpable in Dakar, with small, brightly painted buses zipping past construction cranes, towering minarets and golden beaches sought out by surfers. The neighbourhoods here are as diverse as its people (who speak more than 30 different languages), reflecting a city brimming with creativity and newfound optimism. Home-grown fashion designers, artists and musicians are changing the cultural landscape, with start-ups like Dakar Lives showcasing the city's next generation of innovators.

In addition to its people, Dakar's other great treasure is its landscape. Palm-filled islands are within easy reach of the city centre, and gorgeous beaches lie just south of Dakar. To the north, the bright pink waters of Lac Rose look like something from another planet, while old-fashioned fishing villages conjure up an image of days gone by and offer an enchanting counterpoint to a city ever on the cusp of reinvention.

© DANIEL DI PAOLO

Explore the city's markets for food, flowers, tapestries and jewellery

'Dakar is dazzling to the senses. I love the energy of this city! But when I need a break, I head to the Plage de Yoff or Île de N'Gor to recharge.'

Yvette Diop, graphic designer

UNMISSABLE EXPERIENCES

Spend the day exploring Dakar's vibrant markets. Start off in the city's largest market, the Marché Sandaga. This sprawling downtown bazaar is packed with tapestries, paintings, wood carvings, jewellery, fabrics and countless other treasures. Further west, the Marché Kemel is set in an attractive (rebuilt) Victorian-style building that's full of fruits, vegetables and eye-catching souvenirs – including hand-woven baskets and finely carved masks. The atmosphere here is generally less frenetic than at some other markets. In Médina, the massive and tourist-free Marché Tilene is the go-to place for fabrics, clothing, food products, herbs and traditional medicines. It's an amazingly authentic slice of West African life.

TIME YOUR VISIT

The months of December to February offer the best weather, with cooler temperatures and clear skies. Avoid coming in the rainy season months of July to October. Some places close up shop during these quiet, tourist-free months.

• By Regis St Louis

ITINERARY
Three to four days in Dakar

• Dig your heels in the sand (or go surfing) on **Île de N'Gor**, a small, peaceful island just a short boat ride from the Plage de N'Gor.

• Browse the fine West African artwork at the **Musée Théodore Monod**, Senegal's best art and culture museum.

• Take a day trip up to the **Lac Rose**, a shimmering lake of astonishing pink hues backed by dunes.

• Catch a ferry out to **Île de Gorée**, home to windswept, colonial-era buildings, including the Maison des Esclaves (Slave House), a final point of embarkation for kidnapped Africans during the abominable era of slavery.

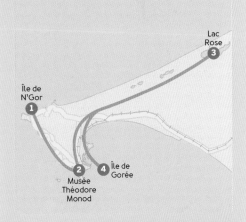

SEATTLE, USA

■■■■ **Smart, progressive and loaded with creative energy,** Seattle is rarely out of the global spotlight. In a city that has a habit of turning home-grown ideas into international brands, Amazon is the current headline-grabber. The world's largest online retailer has radically transformed a vast tract of the Denny Triangle neighbourhood, creating a dense business district of sleek office towers anchored by a trio of innovative glass 'spheres' where workers share office space with 40,000 plants. Nearby, the emblematic Space Needle has received its biggest refurb in over 50 years while, down on the waterfront, a multi-billion-dollar tunnel has replaced an ugly concrete expressway.

08

The 1962 Space Needle
stands tall on the
Seattle skyline

Population: 3.8 million

Language: English

Unit of currency: US dollar

How to get there: Sea-Tac International Airport is located 12km south of downtown. It's one of the top 20 airports in the US, with numerous domestic flights and good direct connections to Asia and a handful of European cities. Amtrak trains head north to Vancouver, Canada; south to Oregon and California; and east as far as Chicago.

'I love Seattle for its beauty and diversity – both of which you get every day at Pike Place Market. For a quick and delicious bite, my favourite go-to is Country Dough.'

Kalyn Kinomoto, communications and marketing associate, Pike Place Market

TELL ME MORE...

The real beauty of Seattle is how it manages to balance its macro-business with its micro-business. For every skyscraper-building billionaire, there's a slew of less-heralded entrepreneurs whose inspired ideas ensure the city remains vital and healthily offbeat. Sure, Amazon hogs the limelight on the national news cycle, but at the grassroots level there are few better cities in which to sample craft beer, peruse thought-provoking public art, or discuss obscure varieties of ethically sourced micro-roasted coffee. Recent cultural uprisings include SoDo Track, a street-art project that's beautified a former utilitarian warehouse district; MarketFront, a funky but historically sympathetic extension to Pike Place Market; and the Nordic Heritage Museum, an underrated cultural

ITINERARY
Two days in Seattle

• At Seattle Center, enjoy the crystallised magnificence of **Chihuly Garden & Glass**, zip up the **Space Needle** for a knockout view of the skyline and end with a journey from Hendrix to Nirvana at the Museum of Pop Culture.

• Spend a morning browsing, tasting, haggling, bantering, dodging fish and getting lost in the **Pike Place Market**.

• See what makes a great art city tick in **Seattle Art Museum**, a skilful amalgamation of tradition and modernism.

• At **Pioneer Square**, kick off with a latte in Zeitgeist Coffee, admire the redbrick architecture around Occidental Sq, and visit the entertaining and educational **Klondike Gold Rush National Historical Park**.

Giant murals line the city's SoDo Track

centre in Ballard that just opened a new campus celebrating the work of Seattle's early Nordic pioneers. Seattle isn't just an excellent place to brighten up your vacation in 2019, it's also a great place to learn something new.

UNMISSABLE EXPERIENCES

• From a cutting-edge art museum to monthly neighbourhood art walks, and a community art wall 'decorated' with chewing gum to a controversial statue of Vladimir Lenin, Seattle is an art city on the rise. For the best public art head north to Fremont (sculptures) or south to SoDo (murals).

• Seattle not only founded some of North America's first brewpubs, it's also led the way in craft distilling and pretty much invented modern coffee culture. Ballard has more micro-breweries per head than any Seattle neighbourhood, Queen Anne is great for cosy coffee shops, while SoDo's Westland Distillery crafts its own single malt whiskey.

TIME YOUR VISIT

Winter is drizzly and dreary. Spring brings a few gorgeous days. July and August are dry and sunny and the best time to visit, although beware of higher prices and bigger crowds. Don't discount balmy September, season of Bumbershoot, Seattle's largest arts and cultural festival, held over the Labour Day long weekend.

• By Brendan Sainsbury

147

09

Drinks at sundown next to Zadar's waterfront

ZADAR, CROATIA

▬▬▬ Zadar has risen from the ashes of its war-ridden past and blossomed into a spirited cosmopolitan city. Wander through the Old Town's warren of bright marble streets to discover cool bars and laidback cafes, ancient Roman ruins, innovative museums and rustic, trattoria-style restaurants. The true phoenix of Zadar's transformation is its imagination-stirring waterfront promenade, where scores of locals gather to listen to the magical chimes of the *Sea Organ* or bask in the mesmeric illuminations of the *Sun Salutation*. Zadar's small stature instantly connects travellers to the local life and culture, with any fears of claustrophobia soon dispelled by those sweeping Adriatic vistas.

Watching the sun go down to the sounds of the *Sea Organ*

© XBRCHX / 500PX

Population: 72,800
Language: Croatian
Unit of currency: Croatian kuna
How to get there: Zadar Airport, a mere 20-minute drive from the Old Town, is well connected to most major European cities. Internal flights are only available from the country's capital Zagreb, but well-serviced bus routes link hotspots such as Split and Dubrovnik.

TELL ME MORE…

While many are drawn moth-like to Split and Dubrovnik, Zadar reaps the benefit of sitting just outside the limelight. This is very much a living city where the energy and bustle of local life is wonderfully juxtaposed with the ancient history hewn into the cityscape. Beyond the urban spaces you'll discover sun-speckled forests, a craggy coastline and jewel-bright waters fringed by the odd pocket of golden sand – it's a corner of paradise but with attitude, which makes it accessible, intriguing and easy to fall in love with.

Zadar is an excellent gateway for exploring the rugged, mountainous wilds of Northern Dalmatia as well as the idyllic and idiosyncratic islets just out of sight over the horizon. A 90-minute drive will transport you to Plitvice National Park, a fantasy world of fluorescent-turquoise lakes animated by a succession of cascading waterfalls. It's an otherworldly beauty that your camera simply can't do justice – so take a day to explore and drink it all in.

ITINERARY
Two days in Zadar

- Start your explorations in grandiose fashion, entering the city via the ostentatious, Renaissance-style **Land Gate**.
- The **People's Square** is the centre of local life, brimming with cafes that are perfect for people-watching.
- Seemingly sprouting from the surrounding plaza, the ancient relics of the **Roman Forum** are fascinating to behold. Peep inside the cavernous St Donatus Church or climb the bell tower of St Anastasia's Cathedral for striking 360-degree views over the Old Town.
- Wander the **waterfront promenade**'s adjacent markets before grabbing some supplies (think ice-cold cocktails and wedges of burek pastry) and heading to the water's edge to sunbathe against the *Sea Organ*'s peaceful backing track.

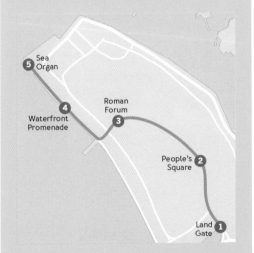

UNMISSABLE EXPERIENCES

- The soul of Zadar can be found where the sea and sun meet the land. Spend a balmy afternoon soaking up the melodic tones of the *Sea Organ*, an intricate system of pipes that uses the ocean waves to create mellifluous tunes. At sunset the solar-powered *Sun Salutation* flickers into action, entrancing locals and tourists with its hypnotic light display.
- Why walk across town when you can take arguably the world's shortest ferry line? For over 800 years the *barkajoli* (boat men) have been rowing people across the 71 short metres of Zadar's harbour.

'Despite its 3000 years of history, Zadar has a modern spirit. Day or night you can swim in the waters off the Old Town listening to the notes of the *Sea Organ* and celebrating the world's best sunset (according to film director Alfred Hitchcock).'

Sandra B, tour guide at
Tours By Locals

TIME YOUR VISIT

April to June is ideal as the weather is warm and prices are still cheap. However, days don't get consistently hot until mid-May. Summer welcomes glorious weather, peak party season and the Full Moon Festival, a folkloric celebration that sees the waterfront bathed in candlelight and the boats lining the quay transformed into floating markets.

- By Louise Bastock

The fluorescent surrounds of Plitvice Lakes National Park are just a 90-minute drive from Zadar

MEKNÈS, MOROCCO

▬▬▬ **The notorious war-mongering sultan** who moved Morocco's capital to Meknès in 1672 would be turning in his grave if he knew how few visitors the city receives today compared with Fez and Marrakesh. Moulay Ismail plundered Marrakeshi palaces and Roman ruins at nearby Volubilis for stone and marble to build thick-set fortifications that still encase the city, giant subterranean food stores and a magnificent *bab* (gate) to outshine even the Blue Gate in Fez. At the heart of the city, Ismail's elaborate mausoleum is a national treasure and in 2018 it emerged from a two-year, top-to-toe restoration, giving travellers more reason than ever to visit this under-appreciated imperial city.

10

Sun hitting the
golden frontage of
Bab el-Mansour

Population: 835,695

Languages: Moroccan Arabic (Darija), French

Unit of currency: Dirham

How to get there: The nearest international airport is Fes-Saïss. From here it's an hour's taxi journey to Meknès, or it's a 30- to 45-minute train ride from central Fez.

TELL ME MORE...

Meknès is a Moroccan city without the tourist filter. Foreign faces aren't all that common here and the dense medina still belongs to locals, who shop and socialise in its souqs and sand-coloured arteries filled with tobacconists, butchers and seamstresses. At dusk, life moves to Pl el-Hedim, which has many of the hallmarks of Marrakesh's Djemaa El Fna but is still the domain of local families, with kids letting off steam and storytellers drawing crowds late into the night with tall Arabian tales.

Few tourists delve deep into Morocco's hinterland, and Meknès has remained under the radar. Yet riads continue to be restored and a relatively luxurious sleep can be had here for much less than in Fez or Marrakesh. Then there's the surrounding Middle Atlas plains: Meknès is the closest jumping-off point for tours of one of Morocco's most important Unesco sights, the Roman ruins of Volubilis. Safe, cheap and entertaining without hassle – Meknès has much to recommend it.

UNMISSABLE EXPERIENCES

• Cross the threshold of Moulay Ismail's mausoleum to explore the hushed chambers within, open to non-Muslims thanks to Ismail's

ITINERARY
Two days in Meknès

• Visit the **Mausoleum of Moulay Ismail** early morning, before the crowds.

• Take a *calèche* (horse-drawn carriage) to the giant royal granary, **Heri es-Souani**, where you can delve into the subterranean vaults and remains of stabling for 12,000 horses.

• **Dar Jamaï Museum** is a beautiful old palace that is worth the small entrance fee as much for the building and gardens as for the traditional craft exhibits inside.

• Pl el-Hedim is the best place to go at dusk to watch the gigantic **Bab el-Mansour** seemingly set on fire by the sinking sun.

• Pack water and a sun hat to explore the mosaic-laden Roman ruins of **Volubilis**.

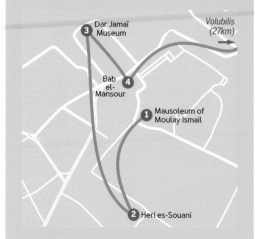

Shopping for
ceramics in
Meknès souqs

© OLEH SLOBODENIUK / GETTY IMAGES

'For a late-afternoon snack, do as locals do and buy freshly baked *sfenj*, the Moroccan doughnut. The most popular vendor is in front of Dar Jamaï Museum.'

Bouchra Jamai, Ryad Bahia owner, Meknès

legacy as the warrior king who paved the way for a united modern Morocco. Non-Muslims are not allowed to approach the tomb itself, but the antechamber is a visual feast of Moroccan craftsmanship.

• Sit with mint tea in hand on one of Cafe Restaurant Place Lehdime's rooftop terraces

as drummers strike up a swansong to the setting sun. At dusk, locals are drawn to Pl el-Hedim like moths to a flame, as the Bab el-Mansour which flanks the plaza is bathed in intense amber light.

TIME YOUR VISIT

From June to August Morocco's parched lands will bake in temperatures as high as 40°C, so plan a trip to coincide with spring (March to May) or autumn (September to November). Wildflowers bring new life to the abandoned ruins of Volubilis in springtime.

• By Lorna Parkes

BEST VALUE
DESTINATIONS

Southern Nile Valley, Egypt / Łódź, Poland /
Great Smoky Mountains National Park, USA / Maldives / Houston, USA /
Argentina / Bangladesh / Albania / Ecuador / Slovenia

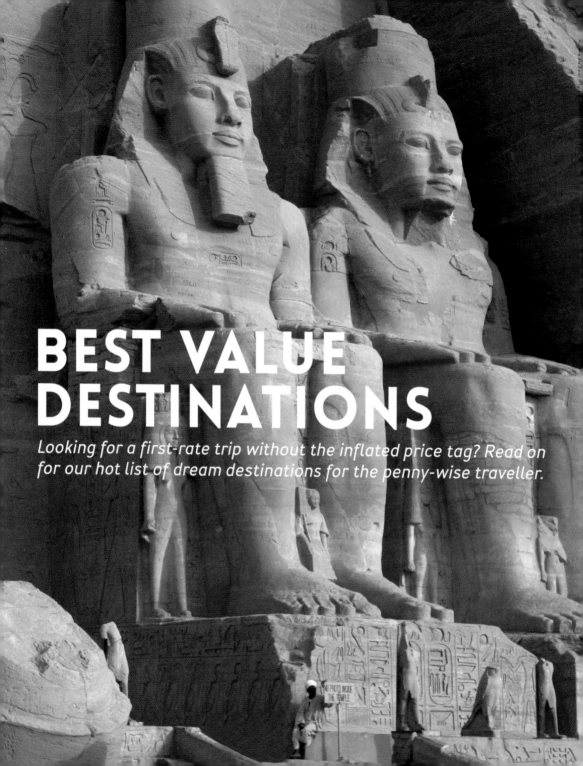

BEST VALUE DESTINATIONS

Looking for a first-rate trip without the inflated price tag? Read on for our hot list of dream destinations for the penny-wise traveller.

THE
TRAVEL
EDIT
BEST IN
TRAVEL
2019

← 1 SOUTHERN NILE VALLEY, EGYPT

Egypt's Southern Nile Valley is the flag-bearer for the country's return to travel's super league, and its near-incomparable historical itinerary represents a superb deal for travellers in 2019. For starters, world-class ancient sites hugging the Nile south from Luxor to Aswan are accessible for a few dollars. If you're on a cruise, food and land transport will be included; otherwise it's easy to make inexpensive arrangements for all but a handful of big-ticket temples and tombs, which are more than worth the admission price themselves. Factor in easy access from Europe and growing visitor numbers and it's a great time for that dream Nile cruise or desert adventure.

A free crossing of one of the monuments of Egypt's modern history, the Aswan Dam, can be had by driving to or from Aswan's airport.

↓ 2 ŁÓDŹ, POLAND

The ambitious post-industrial city of Łódź, the third-largest in Poland, is in a rapid state of transformation. It combines renovation of industrial spaces with bold architectural projects: former factories and other spaces are being transformed into cultural, shopping and entertainment areas. Łódź's EC1 complex continues to take shape and already has a new planetarium, a huge new science and technology centre and a range of exhibition spaces. The Manufaktura shopping and entertainment area is home to the MS2 Museum of Art, a zip line and an artificial beach. And don't miss the remarkable Fabryczna railway station, a work of art with trains.

For a cheap light-adrenaline rush, take a cycle rickshaw down ul Piotrkowska, one of Europe's longest pedestrianised commercial streets.

© AVILLFOTO / SHUTTERSTOCK

↓ 3 GREAT SMOKY MOUNTAINS NATIONAL PARK, USA

Although bizarrely little celebrated outside the USA, the Great Smoky Mountains National Park is no secret, as 10 million annual visitors will attest. This park, which straddles the North Carolina and Tennessee border, is free to enter, which means accessing the view from Clingmans Dome or exploring the atmospheric remains of Cades Cove won't cost you anything more than getting there. It also offers some of the best hiking east of the Mississippi. The park has recovered from the 2016 wildfires and access to the iconic Chimney Tops Trail is almost fully restored, so this is a great time to enjoy a wallet-friendly national park adventure.

Bring bikes and ride the Cades Cove loop road early on Saturday and Wednesday mornings from May through September, when the popular 17.7km circuit is closed to motor vehicles.

THE
TRAVEL
EDIT

BEST IN
TRAVEL
2019

4 MALDIVES

Independent travel is growing in the Maldives as word gets out about a network of inexpensive places to stay on the islands. OK, we're not talking Southeast Asia cheap, but an increasing number of inhabited, non-resort islands have their own locally run guesthouses, bypassing the expensive resort scene and bringing visitors close to what can be the otherwise elusive Maldivian culture. Costs are typically around US$90 per night and meals, diving and other activities can be arranged. Popular islands for independent travellers include Maafushi, Rasdhoo, Thoddoo and Dhigurah, but there are many more, contributing to a growing independent travel scene across the atolls.

The Maldives' public ferry network connects all inhabited islands but does not facilitate travel between the resort islands. Visit www.mtcc.com.mv for timetable information, though check with your guesthouse when you book for confirmation of timings.

© SEAN PAVONE / SHUTTERSTOCK

↑ 5 HOUSTON, USA

Although trips into orbit remain prohibitively expensive, the city from where the moon landings were guided is a great-value place to celebrate the 50th anniversary of the giant leap for mankind. An excellent place to start is Houston's Museum District, which has 19 museums within walking distance: 10 of them are always free and the others offer special free days. The up-and-coming EaDo (East Downtown) district is home to an open-air gallery of murals, and a self-guided tour can take you around this colourful part of town. Houston's diversity inspires its cuisine and great eating needn't mean top-end fine dining. Chinatown, located on Houston's west side, is home to the James Beard Award–nominated Mala Sichuan and Crawfish & Noodles. *Space Center Houston's Historic Mission Control, from where the moon landings were directed, is being refurbished in time for the 2019 anniversary.*

In the past few years, costs for travellers to Argentina have crept up, but the country's efforts to encourage visitors can offer some significant savings. Overseas visitors who pay for their lodging with an international credit card will receive a refund on the 21% rate of Value Added Tax, plus there are savings on visa fees for certain nationalities. The solar eclipse crossing the north of the country is another incentive to visit in 2019, along with Argentina's marvellous mix of world-beating wine, awesome mountain and lake scenery and its crackling-with-life capital Buenos Aires.

Flights to Buenos Aires from London with Norwegian and from Barcelona with Level can reduce the cost of getting to Argentina, but you'll need to factor in baggage costs and other add-ons to be sure you're getting the best fare.

© MATT MUNRO / LONELY PLANET

©ASHIK MASUD / GETTY IMAGES

© LANDSCAPE NATURE PHOTO / SHUTTERSTOCK

↑ 7 BANGLADESH

Bangladesh creates astonishingly few ripples given everything it has to offer. The world's eighth most populated country is home to diverse, exciting cities, Asia's longest beach (and an emerging surf scene) at Cox's Bazar, and the mangroves and wild tigers of Sundarbans National Park. Bangladesh has always been an inexpensive destination for travellers, and Unesco World Heritage sites are waiting to be discovered, such as the open-air museum that is the historic city of Bagerhat, where the Ganges and Brahmaputra rivers meet, and the atmospheric Buddhist ruins at Paharpur. Visitors remain a rarity almost everywhere else, giving Bangladesh an 'out there' feeling that's harder to find in many neighbouring countries. *An unforgettable Bangladesh experience is riding the Rocket, a vintage paddle-wheel steamer, from Dhaka to Barisal, almost certainly for less than the price of lunch where you live.*

→ 8 ALBANIA

Albania has been Europe's final frontier for a while. Here's a pocket of great value hiding in plain sight, with some superb beaches, a unique history and none of the crowds of Montenegro to the north or Greece to the south. The country's exciting food scene celebrates the fruits of its unique local flavours and offers seriously distinctive dining. Although its archaeological sights, such as Apollonia and Butrint, and its one-of-a-kind blend of Balkan, Mediterranean and Italian influences are no secrets, Albania remains a destination where you can hike amid beautiful mountain scenery, stay in tiny and timeless villages and explore the buzzy capital Tirana for far less than pretty much anywhere else in Europe. *Make a good-value day out from Tirana by taking the Dajti Express cable car up the 1611m peak of Mt Dajti. From here, there are hiking trails and picnic spots with commanding views.*

↖ 9 ECUADOR

Want to see the best of South America but short on time? Ecuador is the place for you. Here are green Andean landscapes, colourful colonial towns, Amazon rainforests and Pacific Ocean waves. As you might expect in a small country, buses are quick, plentiful and cheap: hardly anywhere is more than half a day's journey away. Ecuador is home to one of South America's best beach scenes, in the towns north of the city of Guayaquil. Though they're changing fast, the likes of Canoa and Mompiche are still places where you can find a beachside place to crash for a few dollars a night. *Ecuador uses the US dollar as its currency, so there's no need to worry about exchanging money if coming from the US.*

↓ 10 SLOVENIA

This pocket of Europe in miniature is a great-value bet for anyone who's after the continent's highlights but is short on time or funds. In a single day you can tour a Venetian-tinged seaside town, cross Alpine passes and dine by the river in the heart of Ljubljana. But why rush? This is a land of outdoor activities available for much less than you'll pay in other Alpine countries. It is a place of world-class restaurants and wineries, and undiscovered small towns.

Getting around is easy and cheap, and many road and rail journeys are spectacular. Summer brings crowds to lakes Bled and, to a lesser extent, Bohinj, but it's easy to leave them behind.

The train service from Nova Gorica on the Italian–Slovenian border to Jesenice is a beautiful two-hour journey up and over the Julian Alps, linking small villages.
• By Tom Hall

THE
TRAVEL
EDIT

Best new openings / Best new places to stay
Best new food experiences / Best new attractions for kids

BEST NEW OPENINGS

Just because you're a seasoned traveller doesn't mean you have any reason to get jaded in 2019. There are plenty of exciting new openings coming next year to inspire you to plan your next trip.

1 ACADEMY MUSEUM, LOS ANGELES, USA

Discover the art and science of the silver screen in a space that promises a lot more glitz than your average museum. The Academy of Motion Picture Arts and Sciences, the organisation behind the Oscars, has been actively building this collection for more than a decade and it will be shown to the world at the new Museum of Motion Pictures. There'll be everything from scripts to costumes, and highlights include a full-sized shark model from *Jaws*, Shirley Temple's Juvenile Oscar and one very famous pair of ruby slippers.

The red carpet will be out for the museum's grand opening in 2019.

2 THE MUSEUM OF THE FUTURE, DUBAI, UAE

Explore the trends and innovations of tomorrow in one of the world's most futuristic cities. Dubai's Museum of the Future will showcase the design and products we could all be using in the next decade and beyond. It will be the first of its kind in the world and will include a demonstration space where you can see new prototypes in action. The building is set to be another architectural marvel for Dubai – breaking from the city's tradition of eye-catching skyscrapers, the museum will take the shape of a gleaming, silver oval covered in Arabic calligraphy.

Step into the future in late 2019.

→ 3 LITCHFIELD NATIONAL PARK, NORTHERN TERRITORY, AUSTRALIA

The most visited park in Australia's Top End, Litchfield is about to undergo extensive improvements to make it even more attractive to visitors seeking adventure. In total, there will be five new swimming spots, at least three new campgrounds and new routes for both mountain biking and 4WDs. Locals adore this national park and, as it comprises roughly 1500 sq metres of wilderness, there's plenty of it to keep intrepid visitors happy.

All improvements are due to be finished and the park open to the public by March 2019.

← 4 BANGKOK OBSERVATION TOWER, THAILAND

Bangkok's metropolitan skyline is about to light up with a fabulous candle-shaped skyscraper that will be Southeast Asia's tallest observation tower when complete. At 450 metres above the bustling city streets, the tower will be instrumental in efforts to revitalise the waterfront of the Chao Phraya River. As well as gazing out at the city, visitors will get plenty of opportunities to learn about Thai culture and history inside the tower. Some of the profits from ticket sales will go to the local community.

Construction is underway and the tower is expected to be open to the public in 2019.

5 STATUE OF LIBERTY MUSEUM, NEW YORK, USA

If there can only be one icon in the USA, surely Lady Liberty is it. Now she's getting her very own museum to replace the tiny exhibition centre inside the pedestal. Every visitor will get a chance to learn more about her history, delve into the story of her construction and explore the ideals she represents. The freestanding museum – built with sustainable-design principles – will be on Liberty Island, providing sweeping views of the New York City skyline and the famous statue itself. There will be time and space to reflect on the idea of liberty and the key components that keep it protected, such as a free press, elections and access to education. It will be free to enter too.

The museum will open to the masses in 2019.

↑ 6 COMMERCIAL SPACE FLIGHTS

The final frontier may finally be on your doorstep. Four companies are anticipating that 2019 is the year they'll launch commercial flights to space. There's plenty of choice: SpaceX hopes to take two passengers around the Moon, Blue Origin is planning a tourist trip to the edge of space and Virgin Galactic is also working hard to blast off. Perhaps most intriguingly, Russian company Energia wants to fly travellers to the International Space Station and take them on a spacewalk. If you fancy it you'll need a lot of money to go with that keen sense of adventure – the price for a spacewalk comes in at a whopping US$100million.

7 ROE & CO DISTILLERY, DUBLIN, IRELAND

There's no better indicator that Irish whiskey is back in fashion than the fact that drinks giant Diageo, which owns Guinness, has got in on the act. The company is developing its own addition to Dublin's burgeoning distillery quarter with the opening of Roe & Co Distillery in the former Guinness power plant. Alongside the whiskey distillery, an exciting visitor centre is planned for next year. This version of the 'water of life' is named after George Roe, who once owned Ireland's biggest whiskey distillery before it closed, along with many others, during the financial difficulties of the 1920s.

Get a taste of the action from April 2019.

THE
TRAVEL
EDIT
BEST IN
TRAVEL
2019

← 9 SOLAR ECLIPSE TOURS, ARGENTINA AND CHILE

The USA went crazy for a total solar eclipse in 2017 and now there are a wealth of options for travellers who want to chase the next one in July 2019. There are hundreds of different themed tours available to viewing spots in Chile's Atacama and Coquimbo regions, or several provinces in Argentina, including Buenos Aires. Choose from tours with astronomy experts and veteran 'eclipse chasers' or itineraries built around everything from hiking to wine tasting. The highlight, of course, will be a rare opportunity to see the moon totally blocking out the sun.

The solar eclipse is on 2 July 2019 but start booking soon if you want a spot on a dedicated tour.

8 TAMAN TUGU PARK, KUALA LUMPUR, MALAYSIA

Get an experience of a Malaysian rainforest in one of Asia's most modern cities. This green lung in Kuala Lumpur will total 27 hectares and be full of running and walking trails. The ambitious project includes the planting of 4000 ethnic Malaysian trees and 1000 species of flora and fauna. As well as the wild side of nature, there will be a campsite, wetland areas, a jungle walk, an education centre and even an events space to explore. Providing a green refuge to residents and visitors alike, Taman Tugu will also create a huge carbon surplus.

The park will have a phased launch throughout 2019, with the hiking trails open by the start of the year, followed later by the full public facilities.

10 THE CLIMATE HOUSE, OSLO, NORWAY

Klimahuset (Climate House) promises to offer an incredible opportunity for the entire family to learn more about natural and man-made climate change, as well as encouraging people to start taking sustainable action to tackle it. Located in the botanical gardens of Tøyen, the venue will provide a jam-packed activity list daily, including markets, debates and films, a play area for children and some very artistic installations. The structure itself is, naturally, a zero-emissions building.

The Climate House's doors will open in autumn 2019.

• By AnneMarie McCarthy

BEST NEW PLACES TO STAY

Sleep in a bubble, yurt, hostel, boutique city hotel or remote luxury lodge. This year certainly offers up a world full of new choices when it comes to finding memorable places to stay.

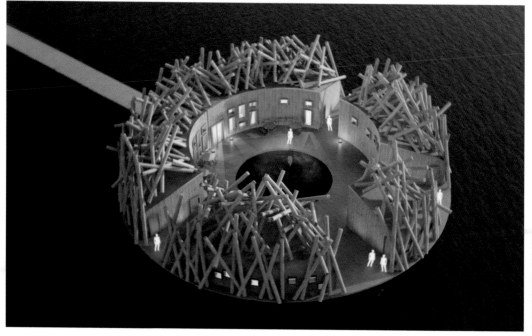

© JOHAN KAUPPI / ARCTIC BATH

↑ 1 ARCTIC BATH, SWEDEN

Although it resembles a mammoth bonfire in waiting, the only thing this giant ring of jumbled logs is going to set on fire is your heart. Floating outstretched in Swedish Lapland's Lule River, this enigmatic structure contains a regulated ice bath (4°C), relaxation rooms and saunas. The complex and the six angular cabins located on the nearby shore are pure Scandi heaven. *The Arctic Bath is a year-round proposition, it floats on the river in summer and is frozen in place during the winter. www.arcticbath.se*

176

THE
TRAVEL
EDIT
BEST IN
TRAVEL
2019

2 AMANYANGYUN, CHINA

When a precious camphor forest and a historic village in Fúzhōu, complete with Ming- and Qing-dynasty homes, were threatened by the rising waters of a new reservoir, luxury brand Aman was persuaded to set out on an incredibly ambitious, decade-long plan to move the whole lot (10,000 trees, buildings and all) some 700km to Shànghǎi's outskirts. The result is this mind-blowing 10-hectare retreat.

A night in one of the 24 suites starts at ¥6000 (US$950). The site includes a spa, cultural centre, kids' club and several restaurants. www.aman.com/resorts/amanyangyun

3 IDEAL ECO-HOSTEL, PARAGUAY

Embrace nature by helping conserve it when staying at this simple eco-hostel in the town of Pilar. It's operated by Para La Tierra, a respected and award-winning NGO that works to protect threatened habitats through scientific research, environmental education

and community engagement. The hostel's proceeds help to fund its work, and guests have the opportunity to volunteer for a range of biodiversity projects.

Dorm beds cost 70,000G (US$14) per night, while a double room will only set you back 150,000G (US$30). ecohostelideal.wixsite.com/idealeco-hostel

↑ 4 THURGAU BUBBLE-HOTEL, SWITZERLAND

Some bubbles never need bursting, and those dotting the Swiss countryside in Thurgau certainly fit this bill. These transparent rooms, equipped with beds that will make you feel as if you're floating through nature, are minimalist bliss. Enjoy starry skies before waking to views of vineyards, orchards, lakes or sweeping gardens. Three of the bubbles have permanent locations, while one rotates every couple of months.

Prices, which include breakfast and a rental bike, start at CHF190 (US$190) per person per night. www.himmelbett.cloud

5 BLACKADORE CAYE, BELIZE

Launched by Leonardo DiCaprio, powered entirely by renewable energy and fed by nothing but rainwater and sunshine, this ambitious eco-resort has plans to regenerate its natural surroundings onshore and off. Health and wellness are at the fore for guests too, so settle in and soak up everything this private Caribbean island has to offer.

Half the island is to be protected as a wildlife reserve and will include a research station on climate change. www.restorativeislands.com

↑ 6 WHITE CITY HOUSE, ENGLAND

The Soho House group has been shaking up the hotel scene in the US and the UK over the past few years, and its latest London offering has reshaped and revolutionised the former BBC Television Centre in White City. The boutique hotel will feature 45 rooms within the legendary building's original Grade II-listed doughnut-shaped core (The Helios), as well as a rooftop pool and extensive club space.

The hotel is part of a major transformation of the site, which includes a cinema, health club and housing. www.whitecityhouse.com

7 GORILLA'S NEST, RWANDA

Staying here won't mean you'll be rolling back, David Attenborough-style, into the embrace of a mountain gorilla in its natural nest, but you will be on the doorstep of the famed *Gorillas in the Mist* story. And you'll be considerably more comfortable and well fed than the beloved nature presenter ever dreamed of.

One&Only Gorilla's Nest is snuggled into the foothills of the Virunga Volcano range and provides easy access to Volcanoes National Park, home to all of Rwanda's gorillas. www.oneandonlyresorts.com

8 THE SIREN HOTEL, DETROIT, USA

Detroit is certainly on the rise, and The Siren Hotel calls attention to it. Fittingly, this 106-room boutique hotel has rejuvenated the derelict, once elegant Wurlitzer building that was built in 1926 as a beacon to the city's success. Nearby, the new QLine streetcar provides quick access to galleries and midtown museums such as the Detroit Institute of Arts. *Rooms, a mixture of reborn grandeur and modern colour and flair, start at US$139.* www.thesirenhotel.com

9 THE TASMAN, HOBART, AUSTRALIA

The Tasman's doors aren't opening until 3 June 2019 but it'll be worth the wait. This luxury hotel is to be set within a group of heritage buildings, including Hobart's grand, Georgian-style St Mary's Hospital, built in the 1800s. The historical elements will be merged with modern artworks and cutting-edge glass and steel structures. *The Tasman will open on Murray St, a short stroll from the harbour, Franklin Sq and Parliament Sq.* www.starwoodhotels.com

↓ 10 EKI CHAT YURT CAMP, KYRGYZSTAN

Feel like truly taking a walk on the wild side? Travel to this traditional yurt camp, set up by the local community in the Eki Chat valley as a launch point for adventurous travellers' trekking and biking forays. It's part of a wider eco-tourism effort in the Ak-Suu region, and the camp aims to be both economically and environmentally sustainable. *The nearest town is Jyrgalan, a 9km hike away. A night here (with breakfast) is 700som (US$10) per person.* jyrgalan.com
• By Matt Phillips

BEST NEW FOOD EXPERIENCES

Food travel is a trend that's only getting hotter, as everyone from gourmands to social-media junkies pack their bags, armed with a list of must-try dining in dreamy destinations. The world is not just your oyster, in 2019 it's a smorgasbord of delicious discovery.

© GUSTAVO VIVANCO

© JASON LOUCAS

↑ 1 MIL, CUSCO, PERU

Fancy some high-altitude dining with views of Inca ruins in a venue run by one of the World's 50 Best chefs? This ode to Andean ancestral cuisine opened in February 2018 and is worth the trek to 3568m above sea level for the astounding scenery and eight-course menu of 'moments', made using ingredients native to the region. Virgilio Martínez (of the acclaimed Central restaurant in Lima) revives ancient ingredients and techniques with modern magic.
To get here, take the flight from Lima to Cusco (approximately 1hr), then it's a 90-min drive. www.milcentro.pe/en

↑ 2 NOMA, COPENHAGEN, DENMARK

The reincarnation of René Redzepi's Copenhagen restaurant launched with much hype and expectation in February 2018. Feted as one of the world's best (certainly the most influential in creating New-Nordic cuisine) restaurants, 'Noma 2.0' has a highly creative, exclusively seasonal menu: Seafood (February to early summer); Vegetable (early summer to early autumn); Game and Forest (early autumn to January).
Follow Noma on social media (@nomacph) for alerts on the next release of seasonal reservations then quickly book online: www.noma.dk

3 MIHARA TOFUTEN, BANGKOK, THAILAND

The new Japanese-influenced tofu restaurant from chef Gaggan Anand (four-time winner of Asia's 50 Best Restaurants for his eponymous Gaggan) is an adventurous, ambitious taste trip. Trading since late-March 2018, Mihara Tofuten brings authentic tofu, *omakase*-style, to Bangkok. A dessert of soya ice cream with white and dark chocolate, matcha and pistachio-flavoured chilled tofu bites will convert sceptics.

For reservations, email resv@mihara tofutenbangkok.com. The 16-course set menu starts from THB3900 (US$122). Wine/ sake pairings are also available on request.

4 LAURA, MORNINGTON PENINSULA, AUSTRALIA

Conceived as a 'love letter' to the beautiful Mornington Peninsula, southeast of Melbourne, this sophisticated merging of food, wine and art on Point Leo Estate enjoys phenomenal sunsets from all angles. Named after a 7m-high cast-iron statue by Spanish sculptor Jaume Plensa, Laura offers views across sparkling Western Port Bay and its sculpture park, one of Australia's largest privately owned collections.

The Mornington Peninsula is best reached by car. Laura is an hour's drive on the Peninsula Link from Melbourne. www.ptleoestate.com.au/laura

↓ 5 'DINE IN THE DOME', THE SUMMERHOUSE, SINGAPORE

The Summerhouse has enchanted diners with its outdoor edible garden since 2017, and now you can luxuriate in a stylish, air-conditioned igloo while eating under the stars on steamy Singapore nights. Each of the three domes has a theme – choose Bohemian, Scandinavian or Lounge – and seats up to eight guests. Wafting lemongrass and wild strawberry add to the rustic romance.

Located in Seletar Aerospace Park, The Summerhouse's 'Dine in the Dome' experience can be booked from S$300 (US$225) per couple: www.thesummerhouse.sg/garden-domes

→ 6 SALT AT PAUL CLUVER, GRABOUW, SOUTH AFRICA

When it comes to food pairing, this restaurant is next level. At Salt, there are six different types of salt placed on every table and each course is paired not only to a specific wine but a specific salt too. Located in the lush Elgin Valley near Cape Town, the restaurant is housed in the Paul Cluver winery – itself known for producing fine chardonnays, rieslings and pinot noirs. Challenge your senses with chefs (and salt aficionados) Craig Cormack and Beau du Toit at the helm.

Salt is in Grabouw, 65km southeast of Cape Town, and is open for breakfast and lunch, serving a two- (R275; US$22) or three-course (R340; US$28) menu. www.cluver.com

7 THE FISHMARKET, EDINBURGH, SCOTLAND

Years in the planning, this new restaurant is a co-creation by Rick Stein's former head chef, Roy Brett, and Gary Welch from Welch Fishmongers. Open since spring 2018, the premises were built from scratch on the grounds of a former fish market on Newhaven Pier, where merchants and fish sellers would ply their trade in the 19th century. The Fishmarket's interior design pays homage to its Victorian heritage and makes an idyllic setting in which to enjoy lobster, oysters and champagne, or a more traditional fish-and-chips supper.

Visit The Fishmarket in spring/summer for fish and chips on the deck with uninterrupted views of the Firth of Forth. www.thefishmarket newhaven.co.uk

8 JORDAN FOOD WEEK, AMMAN, JORDAN

Celebrating the history and diversity of Jordan's food culture, this new festival held in Ras Al Ain, Amman, features 200 producers, including chefs and farmers, showcasing their wares on balmy summer evenings over a week in July. Stroll the stalls, sample home-cooked Jordanian meals from the country's various cities, watch chef demonstrations, take a cooking class and purchase local artisanal produce, all in something of a carnival atmosphere.

Admission to Jordan Food Week costs 2JOD (US$2.80), with special discounts on Amman's Careem taxi app. www.jordanfoodweek.com

THE
TRAVEL
EDIT
BEST IN
TRAVEL
2019

↑ 9 MOSS, BLUE LAGOON, ICELAND

Already popular with visitors seeking outdoor thermal bathing bliss, Iceland's Blue Lagoon now offers a hotspot for foodies, Moss Restaurant, within its new luxury Retreat hotel. Since April 2018, diners have been able to enjoy traditional Icelandic dishes (splurge on the seven-course tasting menu at the 10-seat Chef's Table), views of volcanic landscapes and wine from a unique, multi-hued lava cellar, frozen since 1226.

The Blue Lagoon is handily located between Reykjavík and Keflavík International Airport. There are hourly bus transfers between both. www.retreat.bluelagoon.com/restaurant

10 THE CIVILISATIONS SUPPERCLUB, LONDON

This supper club series, launched in March 2018, is held in various extraordinary venues around London. Expect thematic food, music and stories focused on history and culture, along the lines of 'An Arabian Feast: 1001 Flavours, Sounds & Stories from Syria', which was held in Leighton House's Grand Studio; and '13th-century Syrian Feast', inspired by dinners that were held on the riverbanks of ancient Barada and the Euphrates, which took place at the London Canal Museum.

The supper club is an initiative by Sakbeh, a food catering and events company. www.sakbeh. co.uk/pages/civilisations

• By Karyn Noble

BEST NEW ATTRACTIONS FOR KIDS

Each year the world seems to provide more and more amazing experiences for the younger generation. Here are just some of the new attractions that children will love to explore in 2019.

↗ 1 LEGO HOUSE, BILLUND, DENMARK

What's not to love about the 'Home of the Brick'? Firstly, it's an entirely Lego-themed museum and experiential space located where the Lego story all began. Secondly, it's very easy on the eye (we're in the home of cool design, after all). Thirdly, it's specifically constructed to focus on learning through play, with different zones for creativity, cognitive ability, emotion and social play. And for those who want to be inspired in their building, there's a Masterpiece Gallery and History Collection to explain how it all began. Lastly there's plenty to explore both within and outside the ticketed zones so it needn't break the family bank. A must for all fans of the humble brick, be they big or small, girl or boy.

Everything you need to know (including updates on new events), plus some fascinating insights on the whole project, is at www.legohouse.com.

BEST NEW ATTRACTIONS FOR KIDS

THE
TRAVEL
EDIT
BEST IN
TRAVEL
2019

↙ 2 LIVE WIRE PARK, VICTORIA, AUSTRALIA

If you and your kids love nature (and adrenaline rushes) then family-owned, environmentally friendly Live Wire Park should be on your collective bucket list. Billing itself as the 'ultimate elevated adventure', the park allows children aged between seven and 15 to take part in the Short Circuit, where they have to complete 26 activities involving obstacle courses and suspended trails through the Otway treetops. Once everyone's heart rates have returned to normal, you can chill out on the beach in the beautiful coastal town of Lorne on the Great Ocean Road.

Book now at livewirepark.com.au.

3 SPORTS LEGENDS EXPERIENCE, INDIANAPOLIS, USA

Based at the Children's Museum, this immersive experience encompasses health education, physical fitness and sports history for an active day out. Families can shoot hoops, be inspired by the stories of famous sports legends or work together on a pit-stop challenge (to highlight just three of the 15 activities available). For children over seven there's also the chance to climb up inside the 25ft 'Tree of Sports'. And when everyone needs a break from sports there are five floors of the Children's Museum to explore, all on the same ticket.

Check out the options for different ages with Varsity Team, Junior Varsity and Little Sports Legends. www.childrensmuseum.org

4 KIDZANIA, DOHA, QATAR

There's no denying that children love the chance to play at being grown-ups and they can do this to their heart's content in the interactive city of KidZania. Its outpost in Doha is part of an expansion of 12 new sites, so there will soon be a total of 36 venues around the world where your children can try more than 100 different careers and buzz around a safe city that's created just for them. Children under eight need to be accompanied by an adult so it could be just the place to find some career advice of your own.

A list of all KidZania locations with links to websites can be found at www.kidzania.com.

5 DIPPY ON TOUR, AROUND THE UK

The former centrepiece of London's Natural History Museum needs no introduction. Although his days welcoming visitors to the Hinzte Hall may be over, the world-famous cast of a diplodocus – affectionately known as Dippy – is now taking a leisurely tour around the UK. His route takes in various towns and cities including the Ulster Museum in Belfast, Glasgow's Kelvingrove Art Gallery & Museum, Newcastle and Cardiff, and he's settling for a few months in each, giving people plenty of time to view this amazing specimen of natural history and learn all about his time on Earth.

Follow Dippy via the 'Take Part' section of the Natural History Museum website: www.nhm.ac.uk

6 MONOPOLY MANSION, KUALA LUMPUR, MALAYSIA

For most children (and many adults), staying somewhere different is half the fun of travelling. Add to that a hotel themed around a world-famous board game that graces the shelves of most houses in the Western world and the excitement levels are heading straight past Go. Boasting a 1920s Great Gatsby feel, this five-star, 255-room hotel – and world's first Monopoly hotel – may be better suited to older children (have you tried to play Monopoly with a five-year-old?) but all ages need to come ready to build their property empire and get rich quick.

The Monopoly Mansion is set to open its doors in the spring of 2019.

↑ 7 SLOTH PRESERVE, ARENAL VOLCANO NATIONAL PARK, COSTA RICA

The humble sloth is a fascinating creature, both for its looks and its survival techniques. And if you're taking your kids to Costa Rica, chances are that watching wildlife is high on your list of things to do. So take it to the next level with a visit to this luxury resort in the Arenal Volcano National Park. The Nayara Hotel has planted 300 cecropia trees to create a preserve where the canopy is now home to 15 sloths and counting. Observing the animals at work isn't exactly taxing but if you want to increase the family's activity levels then the resort also offers bird watching, canopy tours and a lava field walk.

www.arenalnayara.com

8 DRIVING SCHOOL, TAYTO PARK, IRELAND

If life in the fast (or even slow) lane appeals to your children, they will love the chance to be proper drivers at Tayto Park's new driving school, opening April 2019. Not surprisingly, it's sponsored by a car manufacturer but what children might not expect is that they take away their own 'driving licence' at the end of the day. There are lessons in how to drive and then a chance to take to the road with 20 other young drivers. When it's time for a pit stop there's the rest of the theme park and zoo to explore.

Tayto Park is in County Meath, 30 minutes' drive from Dublin. www.taytopark.ie

9 STAR WARS GALAXY'S EDGE, USA

When you bring Disney and *Star Wars* together magical things happen for all lovers of a galaxy far, far away. Opening first in California's Disneyworld Resort and then in Walt Disney World, Florida, this attraction is still in development but we do know that it will be themed around Batuu, a remote outpost on the 'Galaxy's Edge' and visitors will be able to fly the Millennium Falcon. Feeling as if they are actually part of the *Star Wars* story is a pretty epic draw for fans small (and big!) so we're sure a visit to Galaxy's Edge is going to need all the 'beat the queues' intelligence you can get.

Keep an eye on the official Disney site for updates. disneyparks.disney.go.com

↓ 10 BEAR GRYLLS ADVENTURE, BIRMINGHAM, UK

If you have teens, this new £20-million (US$27-million) indoor adventure centre could be the perfect way for the whole family to bond over a set of collectively terrifying experiences. In the spirit of survival specialist Bear Grylls you will be able to try climbing routes inspired by famous terrains such as Mt Everest and Yosemite's El Capitan, plus high ropes and diving of both the sky and water varieties. Then there's the Basecamp where you will learn the core skills needed for survival, including a secret 'face your own fear' challenge. Scared?

Open in autumn 2018 for those aged 13+ only. www.beargryllsadventure.com

• By Imogen Hall

TOP TRENDS

Dark skies / Augmented attractions / Road trips go electric

My DNA and me / Getting off the touristed path

DARK SKIES

As Earth grows ever more populous and cities expand, opportunities for humanity to look up at the rest of the universe decrease. Across the planet, travellers are now seeking out the world's last-remaining dark places where they can get a clear, unpolluted view of the stars.

The twinkling span of the Milky Way. A meteor streaking across the horizon. There is something primal about watching the night sky. And nothing inspires more wanderlust than pondering the vastness of the universe underneath a sky full of constellations. Sadly, visual access to the night sky has, over the past century, become increasingly rare.

According to research by the Light Pollution Science and Technology Institute, 80% of Earth's land mass suffers from light pollution, while for 99% of people in Europe and the USA the night sky is obscured by artificial lighting.

In 2001, the International Dark-Sky Association set up a programme to award destinations working to preserve their dark skies, and astrotourism has been a growing trend since. In 2017, about seven million people travelled across the USA to see the total solar eclipse and similar pilgrimages are expected in South America this year when another eclipse will temporarily darken a swath of the continent.

Thanks to growing awareness and increasing numbers of designated dark-sky parks, travellers can combine seeing a new place with getting under the stars, whether on a stargazing tour, at a star party or while sipping a glass of bubbly atop a volcano. Many of the world's great observatories are open to visitors, some offering short astronomy courses and stargazing evenings.

DARK-SKY PARKS

Designated dark-sky places, such as the parks and communities certified by the International Dark-Sky Association, are among the best places to see the sky free from light pollution.

← SOUTHWEST USA

The clear, dry southwestern USA has a great collection of dark-sky places, including the world's first designated dark-sky park at Natural Bridges in Utah; the dark-sky city of Flagstaff, Arizona; the Cosmic Campground in New Mexico; and the Grand Canyon, which hosts an annual star party in June.

JAPAN

In 2018, Japan was awarded its first accredited dark-sky place: Iriomote-Ishigaki National Park in Okinawa Prefecture. The 406-sq-km park covers the remote sub-tropical Yaeyama Islands off Japan's southern coast and provides the best stargazing in the country.

NORTHERN BRITAIN

Some of Europe's darkest skies can be found over the remote parts of northern Britain, including the country's first designated dark-sky park, Northumberland National Park and Kielder Water & Forest Park. Go Stargazing (www.gostargazing.co.uk), run by a former Kielder Observatory volunteer, has recommendations for stargazing spots and events around the UK.

So what compels us to go out of our way to get a glimpse of the universe? 'A hundred thousand generations of homo sapiens before us saw the Milky Way every night,' says J Thomas Beckett, board chair of Utah's Clark Planetarium. 'It's in our DNA. But then we lit up the outdoors and literally lost sight of it. Astrotourists are reconnecting with something that has a deep, primitive meaning to humans.'

No matter how you choose to experience the night sky, astrotourism offers a glimpse through history and an important and fascinating sense of perspective about our place in the universe.

• By Megan Eaves

AURORA HUNTING

The natural sky displays aurora borealis (Northern Lights) and aurora australis (Southern Lights) are elusive and beautiful events that are only observable close to the planet's poles.

→ SCANDINAVIA

September to April is the best time to try for a glimpse of the aurora from the European Arctic. Take your pick from the northern reaches of Scandinavia, where dedicated tours and accommodations deliver beautiful views of the Northern Lights.

STEWART ISLAND, NEW ZEALAND

Head to Stewart Island in New Zealand from March to September to view the lesser-known aurora australis. The auroras here are said to have given the island its Māori name – Rakiura, or 'glowing skies'.

ASTRO-EXPERIENCES

There are stargazing experiences of all stripes, whether you want to visit a remote corner of the world, see a once-in-a-lifetime event or stargaze from a luxury hotel.

STELLAR TOURS

Astro.Tours (www.astrotours.co) offers immersive astronomy tours led by scientists and donates a percentage of its profits to research. *Sky & Telescope magazine (www. skyandtelescope.com) provides limited-number tours to astronomical destinations each year, led by its editors and experts.*

STARRY YURT STAY

A trip to remote Central Asia or Mongolia offers a DIY approach to night-sky travel combined with the opportunity to stay in a yurt and connect with the local culture.

© SPREEPHOTO.DE | GETTY IMAGES | MOMENT RF

OBSERVATORIES

Often located in dark, clear-sky places atop peaks and volcanoes, observatories offer a double opportunity for learning the science of modern astronomy and naked-eye stargazing.

MAUNA KEA, HAWAII

Hawaii's incredible 4200m Mauna Kea peak houses the world's largest observatory for optical astronomy. Visitors can use on-site telescopes and attend stargazing sessions at the clear-sky summit.

CANARY ISLANDS

Far away from the light pollution of mainland Europe, the Canary Islands' international observatories at Teide on Tenerife and Roque de los Muchachos on La Palma are open to visitors for guided tours and stargazing sessions.

CRUISES

Due to its lack of light pollution, the open sea is a great place for stargazing. Hurtigruten (www.hurtigruten.co.uk) runs an astronomy cruise with onboard lectures. The route runs the entire length of the Norwegian coast from Bergen to far beyond the Arctic Circle. Princess Cruises (www. princess.com) offers stargazing nights that are led by an astrophysicist.

STARGAZING HOTELS

Book into a night-sky hotel, such as Elqui Domos (www.elquidomos.cl) in Chile, where rooms come with telescopes and sky-view domes. Baines' Camp (www. sanctuaryretreats.com) in Botswana offers 'sky beds' and 'star baths' on open-air decks; and in Scotland, Ackergill Tower (www. ackergilltower.com) has a treehouse in which you can view the stars from your bed.

AUGMENTED ATTRACTIONS

VR, AR. Unless you've been living under a rock for the past few years, you've heard of virtual and augmented reality, technologies that have made the leap from sci-fi to smartphone. And now they're transforming every stage of the travel experience.

First, let's recap: VR refers to a computer simulation of an environment that you can experience through the senses – principally sights and sounds but there's more to come – and interact with. Doing so requires a headset, which is sometimes paired with more exotic forms of interface such as sensor-laden gloves. AR works differently, superimposing digital information on a user's view of the world through a device such as a smartphone, thus adding an extra layer to reality.

After years of predictions about these technologies eating the world, followed by a few false dawns (hello and goodbye, Google Glass), it does now feel as if we're past the point of no return; the tentacles of VR and AR reach well beyond the limits of geeksville, ensnaring not only the entertainment industry, but also domains as diverse as retail, healthcare and manufacturing to name but three. And then, of course, there's travel.

Armchair travel has entered a new golden age thanks to an explosion of apps offering immersive 360-degree content: just slip your smartphone into a headset, or don a more powerful standalone version, and you can tour destinations, attractions and hotels without ever leaving the house. Heck, you can even visit NASA's Curiosity rover on the surface of Mars if you feel like it (alas, you can't book a weekend break on the red planet just yet).

But the potential of VR and AR becomes even more brain-liquefying when you ponder how they might enhance a trip as it unfolds.

• By James Kay

BRINGING HISTORY TO LIFE

Good storytelling is what makes a great museum, so no wonder cultural institutions have embraced the potential of VR and AR, the next best thing to time travel.

WASHINGTON, DC, USA

There's nothing fusty about the Smithsonian National Museum of Natural History's 1881 Bone Hall (naturalhistory.si.edu). Examine the exhibits there by using the Skin & Bones app to see skeletons escape their mounts and extinct species come to life.

WATERFORD, IRELAND

Meet the mighty warlords who founded Ireland's oldest city, thanks to a magic combination of real-life actors, holograms and VR at the King of the Vikings experience at the Waterford Museum of Treasures (www. kingofthevikings.com).

DARWIN, AUSTRALIA

Relive one of the darkest days in Australia's history in real time at the Royal Flying Doctor Service (rfdsdarwin. com.au) attraction in Darwin. It features a spectacular VR re-creation of the February 1942 bombing of the city's harbour, as well as a 55-seat hologram cinema.

WHEN WORLDS COLLIDE

Bringing history to life doesn't have to happen in a museum, of course. You'll also find examples of these technologies in the open, where they add a whole new dimension to a trip.

↓ PARIS, FRANCE

Fancy a peak at Paris the day after the 1789 revolution? Gawp at panoramic, historically accurate views of the city as it once was through a pair of VR-enabled telescopes, or Timescopes (timescope.co), installed near Pont d'Arcole and Place de la Bastille.

SPAIN AND GREECE

Join a guided walking tour of Seville, Barcelona, Athens or Ephesus with Past View (www.pastviewexperience. com) to try a pair of smartglasses that superimpose re-creations of historical scenes on the locations where they actually happened.

SITES ACROSS ENGLAND

Conjure up virtual guides and unlock intriguing stories at a dozen heritage-heavy sites, from Durham Cathedral to Chester Roman Amphitheatre and Maritime Greenwich, with Explore England's Historic Cities app (www.heritagecities.com/ stories).

PARALLEL UNIVERSES

There are one-off uses which demonstrate that, just like AR and VR, the human imagination knows no bounds.

DUBAI, UAE

Vertigo-proof visitors to the 125th level of Dubai's Burj Khalifa – the world's tallest building – can embark on a virtual climb to the top wearing suction gloves, then freefall 828m to the ground.

TOKYO, JAPAN

Whereas other carriers use VR soberly to showcase their network of destinations, First Airlines (firstairlines.jp) has a more radical approach: it 'flies' headset-wearing passengers to New York, Paris, Rome or Hawaii without leaving Tokyo.

VR AS THE STAR

Though these technologies are about enhancing reality, they're often used to escape it entirely. These attractions make VR the star, offering cutting-edge immersive experiences.

VIRTUAL ROLLERCOASTERS, WORLDWIDE

VR has colonised theme parks in various guises, but none more spectacularly than the virtual rollercoaster, which pairs physical thrills with fantasy worlds. You'll find them at Six Flags throughout the US, Legoland in Malaysia, Germany and Florida, and many others.

↑ OUT-OF-HOME VR EXPERIENCES, WORLDWIDE

Companies such as IMAX VR (imaxvr.imax.com), The Void (www.thevoid. com) and Zero Latency (zerolatencyvr.com) are rolling out a new class of entertainment venue: warehouse-like spaces designed solely for state-of-the-art, free-roaming, multiplayer VR games. All three businesses have growing global networks.

ROAD TRIPS GO ELECTRIC

Classic road trips are evolving into something more fully charged. As countries and rental companies make the electric leap, choosing to reduce your carbon footprint with an EV has never been easier.

THE EV REVOLUTION IS COMING

Electric vehicles (EVs) are a technology on the verge. However, the mass adoption of this eco-friendly option has faced a classic chicken-and-egg struggle: what comes first, EV owners or widespread public charging stations? Travellers who want to take one for a spin while on vacation face an additional barrier, as many rental-car companies have been slow to introduce EVs as an option.

There's hope on the horizon, though. Many countries are rolling out ambitious plans to install charging stations, while car companies that produce EVs are adding infrastructure to support their uptake. Though EVs are often seen as more practical for urban exploration, the addition of chargers along rural routes has brought opportunities to get out on the open road. While in many countries an electric road trip is a distant dream, there are a number of EV-ready destinations that might surprise you.

Whether you're trying to go green or want something new, an EV road trip is the perfect adventure for travellers who love a challenge. So, as the stars align for an electrically charged getaway, be part of a group of pioneers hitting the road without the drone of a gas-guzzling engine.

EMBRACE YOUR RANGE ANXIETY

In the age of GPS and Google Maps, it's becoming harder and harder to take a wrong turn. Sure, you'll get to your destination faster, but you might miss out on the sort of adventure that comes from (accidentally) taking the road less travelled.

EV drivers often experience 'range anxiety': the fear of being too far away from a charging station. While that's natural, even among the experienced, once you turn that anxiety into the fuel for your trip, the thrill of the charging chase can begin, even along a scenic detour.

Planning for an EV adventure is a challenge that comes with its own rewards. EV drivers look after their own and there are plenty of online resources, forums and apps mapping EV chargers around the world. When you get behind the wheel of an EV, you're joining a community ready to explore the world in a new way, and they will help you do the same.

IT'S NOT ABOUT THE DESTINATION...

Not all EV chargers are created equally and you may find yourself stopped for a while – even hours – to recharge. Take a cue from your vehicle and rest up a while, perhaps in a place you never imagined. Public chargers have been rolled out differently by cities, countries and businesses. You could find yourself outside a college campus, at a spa along a stunning coastline, or in an out-of-the-way strip mall in a town you've never heard of.

EV road-tripping will force you to stop and smell the roses, so ignore anyone who tells you this is a downside. In reality, this presents the perfect opportunity to explore someplace you may never have stopped if a petrol station was handy. Your EV has made you a new kind of adventurer – embrace it.

• By Alex Butler

TEN GREAT PLACES FOR ELECTRIC ROAD-TRIPPING

WEST COAST GREEN HIGHWAY, NORTH AMERICA
Cruise from British Columbia to California, waving to fellow EV drivers along the way.

NATIONAL TOURIST ROUTE HARDANGERVIDDA, NORWAY
Journey from Bergen to see the waterfalls and mountains in Hardangervidda National Park.

BARBADOS
Leave no beach untouched while making the most of the island-wide charging system.

MADEIRA, PORTUGAL
Exploring Madeira in an EV? Find one that can fit your hiking gear and a surfboard.

UNITED ARAB EMIRATES AND OMAN
Hit all seven emirates and stop in Muscat and Sohar without worrying about your charge.

GOLDEN ROUTE, JAPAN
Take this busy route past Mt Fuji from Tokyo to Kyoto without adding to the fumes.

NORTH COAST 500, SCOTLAND
Travel the Scottish Highlands – but you still can't get behind the wheel after sampling from the local distilleries!

QUEENSLAND'S ELECTRIC SUPER HIGHWAY, AUSTRALIA
Cruising from Cairns to Coolangatta has never been such a breeze.

ROUTE 66, USA
Like Bob Dylan before it, this US classic has gone electric (but with more public blessing).

BLACK FOREST, GERMANY
Drive into a fairy tale on one of the most environmentally friendly routes in Germany.

TOP
TRENDS
BEST IN
TRAVEL
2019

ELECTRIC
VEHICLE
PARKING
ONLY

MY DNA AND ME

In a world where we're increasingly virtually connected, we can feel disengaged from our roots. But thanks to developments in genetic testing and accessible historical records, travellers are finding it easier than ever to pack a bag and journey back to their origins, forging stronger connections with people and cultures along the way.

All travellers are curious – it's what keeps the wanderlust alive. The recent rise in home DNA kits has spurred on explorers to delve into their cultural heritage, planning trips around the movements of their ancestors before them.

Retracing your ancestors' footsteps is an adventure replete with surprises. Be prepared to uncover corners of the globe you never knew existed, or travel to familiar destinations and see them in a new light. This very personal journey could find you on a ferry to a remote Scottish island in search of a long-lost relative, or standing in front of your great grandmother's childhood home in the centre of New York City. Be they new experiences or not, a personal connection can't help but change your perspective of a destination, and discovering kinship with new people and cultures will also give you an invaluable travel souvenir: a new-found identity.

Of course, the trail may not always be fruitful, but the quest is part of the fun – who knows what exciting experiences you may have and who you may meet along the way? In a bid to find travel inspiration in the past, we asked six members of the Lonely Planet family to take a DNA test and plan a trip based on the results. Wherever they end up, we're sure it'll be one interesting ride.

• *By Maria McKenzie*

→ PORTUGAL

Right after finding out my DNA results and discovering I have Portuguese blood in me, I booked a ticket to Portugal to explore this beautiful land my ancestors once walked. When you discover that a part of you is found in a place you have never been to, you automatically feel a pull to it. It's like going on the ultimate global treasure hunt of self discovery.

• Kristen Sarah, Canadian, Lonely Planet Trailblazer, blogger and YouTuber

41% Italian, 21.4% broadly European, 17% British and Irish, 9% French and German, 6% Norwegian, 3% Iberian, 1% Balkan, 0.4% Finnish, 1% Western Asian and North African, 0.1% East Asian and Native American, 0.1% Sub-Saharan African.

→ GEORGIA

I've long heard rumours of having distant relatives living somewhere in the Caucasus. The more I read up about Georgia, the more I spot photographs of local people who have a degree of – how should I put this? – ruddy-cheeked, wavy-haired familiarity. There's much I'd love to experience in the country, from sci-fi architecture in Soviet-era Black Sea resorts to winemaking traditions that can be traced back to the Romans. Finding out my results has underscored how the human urge to travel has made so many of us more diverse than we might realise.

• Peter Grunert, British, Group Editor Lonely Planet magazines

72% North & West European, 24% Irish, Scottish and Welsh, 2.2% Iberian, 1.1% West Asian

↑ ESTONIA

Equipped with my new-found Eastern European genealogy, I'd love to brace the easterly winds and pay a visit to cities I've had on my bucket list for some time – Tallinn and St Petersburg. Being mixed race, I had always identified my heritage as being half of one thing and half of another. My results have reshaped seeing heritage as only two family histories – it's eye-opening to see that there are many nationalities in my DNA. It's reminded me how much of the world is, in fact, 'mixed', and will continue to be as long as people keep travelling and experiencing new cultures.

• Christina Webb, British, Lonely Planet Assistant Editor
57.8% South Asian, 33.6% Irish, Scottish and Welsh, 4.4% English, 4.2% Eastern European

↑ SPAIN

The biggest surprise in my DNA results was the 17% Iberian Peninsula portion. None of the amateur genealogists in my family have identified an ancestor from Spain or Portugal, so I have some work to do! I definitely plan to travel to the region and hopefully learn more about my ancestry first-hand. It's interesting to have a better sense of the place and history where my ancestors came from – though their descendents are mostly in the US now, the geopolitical, social, and historic forces that drove migration, trade, and marriage across cultures help explain how connected the world has become.

• Valerie Stimac, American, Lonely Planet Local
33% Eastern European, 29% Western European, 17% Iberian Peninsula, 16% Southern European, 4% Great Britain

← JAPAN

I had 1% Korean Japanese show up in my DNA results. My entire family was shocked – we don't know if it was my mother's side (mainly Middle Eastern) or my father's (Eastern European/Russian). Now that I know my family roots, there's a different sense of what makes me, me. I hope to see similarities between myself, my interests and habits, and the locals I meet. I may walk down a street and distant cousins may walk past me; I've never felt that before.

• Siya Zarrabi, Canadian, Lonely Planet Trailblazer, travel videographer and blogger

46% Western Asian, 49% European (Ashkenazi Jewish), 2% Iberian, 1% Korean Japanese, 1% North African, 0.5% South Asian, 0.5% Native American

← ENGLAND

After looking into where my French DNA came from, I discovered the French individual who married into the family traced back through London to Colchester, a small city that is known as England's first Roman town. I had visited London many times but had never been out to the eastern side of England where this family resided. It turns out that Colchester is where my family emigrated from in the mid-1800s to join pioneers heading west in the United States.

• Mike Nelson, American, Lonely Planet Director of Ecommerce

32% Western Europe, 67% Great Britain, 1% Scandinavia

GETTING OFF THE TOURISTED PATH

It's no secret that some of the world's most amazing destinations are feeling the tourism squeeze. But that's no reason to stay put: as communities cope with travellers' all-too-loving embrace, being a good tourist just means getting strategic about where to go and when.

Every traveller is on a journey, though it's becoming clearer that some paths are so well trodden that they're at risk of wearing out. Even when we try to venture off the tourist track it can be hard not to bump into others doing the same thing. But that doesn't mean it's time to put away your packing cubes and ignore your itchy feet; it's just a new opportunity to consider your impact on the places you cherish.

There are many ways to spread the travel love, and beating the crowds doesn't mean skipping the iconic spots. Sustainable travel can come in many forms. Stay in an underexplored neighbourhood in a must-see city and you'll get to live like a local and support the community. Skip the day trip – which will only leave you without a feel for the place – and spend more time in local shops and cafes, picking up some incredible, and meaningful, souvenirs.

Alternatively, be a true explorer and take a chance on an unfamiliar destination. Who knows? You may have found travel's next hidden gem. With a bit of thought and consideration,

your next trip won't leave you feeling like just one tourist among the masses, overwhelming the local community. Travel can be a force for good – help keep it that way.

• *By Alex Butler*

ALTERNATIVE MUST-SEE SIGHTS

People journey to popular places such as Machu Picchu and Angkor Wat because they have to be seen to be believed. But many others attractions will astonish you – and give you a bit more breathing space.

→ HUMAYUN'S TOMB, INDIA

In Delhi, about 200km from the Taj Mahal, is another awe-inspiring example of Mughal architecture: Humayun's tomb. While it has a less-romantic backstory, it's thought to have inspired the design of the other more famous – and crowded – site.

← CANADA'S NATIONAL PARKS

The US national parks are undoubtedly awesome, but head north to Canada, where, with a fraction of the visitors, you can often explore the wilderness on your own.

UNDERRATED SPOTS

Revel in the questioning looks you get when you tell your friends you're heading to these less-travelled destinations. They'll be asking you for tips in no time.

THE FAROE ISLANDS, DENMARK

Looking for the natural wonders and undeniable coolness that makes Nordic countries irresistible? Well, there's one spot you might have overlooked. Home to soaring cliffs, epic coastlines and even a Michelin-starred restaurant, the Faroe Islands are ready and waiting to be explored.

TORONTO, CANADA

Toronto is often outshone by hip Montréal and stunning Vancouver, which is a shame, because it's one of the most multicultural city's on the planet. Take a tour of the world in a day – with some help from the friendly locals who call it home.

LJUBLJANA, SLOVENIA

Unlike some European capitals, Slovenia's top city is still begging to be explored. Ljubljana serves up the canals and castles you desire, with a huge expanse of green space in which to stretch your legs. Plus there are plenty of cafe terraces, alternative clubs and arty hangouts.

© JURGAR / GETTY IMAGES

STAYING IN A LOCAL SUBURB

Thanks to the growth of homestays, hip hostels and boutique hotels, there's no need to stay in the city centre. Get away from the casual tourists and explore neighbourhoods that make a city unique.

AMSTERDAM

Amsterdam is more than the Red Light District. See its many facets first-hand by

TOP OFF-SEASON DESTINATIONS

There's no need to miss the big hitters, just visit when the crowds have gone.

↓ VENICE, ITALY

To truly admire the beauty of Venice, you need to step back and take a good look. That means skipping the summer. Packing a jacket in your luggage will be worth the extra space you'll get on the streets.

TURKEY

Whether soaking up the sun at a coastal resort or hitting up the hippest 'hoods in sprawling Istanbul, avoid the stress of big crowds by visiting in the off-season.

← SOUTH AFRICA

Travelling in low-season means you won't enjoy the full heat but you'll benefit from discounted safaris and less-crowded wineries. Trust us, your chenin blanc will taste better with fewer people around.

sauntering out of the centre and into vibrant districts such as artsy Westerpark or diverse Indische Buurt.

LONDON

London's size means that hopping from neighbourhood to neighbourhood, like hip Hackney or creative Camden, is like finding yourself in a new city. Since riding the Tube is already a quintessential London experience, there's no excuse not to get out and explore.

INDEX

MAKING
BEST IN TRAVEL

Of all the amazing places and travel experiences on the planet, how do we choose the most exciting for the year ahead? It's a decision we do not take lightly. Read on for an overview of how the magic happens.

1 THE SURVEY

The annual *Best in Travel* survey is sent to the whole Lonely Planet family – every staff member, over 200 travel writers, bloggers, our publishing partners and more. In it we ask LPers to share their expertise on places and travel trends that they predict will be buzzing in the year ahead.

2 THE TRAVEL HACK

We also organise brainstorming events in Lonely Planet offices the world over – from Běijīng to Buenos Aires. This is when we come together to discuss the subject that inspires us the most: travel. Where have

we been? What are we excited about? Which destinations are doing something special? Amid a flurry of Post-it notes and coffee cups, the Travel Hacks produce hundreds of ideas.

3 THE DESTINATION EDITORS

The results of the survey and Travel Hacks produce a longlist of more than a thousand ideas. This is then reviewed by the Destination Editors – Lonely Planet's regional experts, a varied bunch of travel geeks with hundreds of thousands of air miles between them. They help whittle down the list to the very best places.

4 THE PANEL

A shortlist of the best ideas is then sent to a panel of travel experts. These are six people who live and breathe travel in their everyday lives. They scrutinise each idea and score them out of 100 for topicality, excitement and 'wow' factor.

5 THE FINAL LIST

When the panel results are in, the list is finalised and shared with a trusted handful of people at Lonely Planet until October when, finally, the selection of the best places and travel trends to experience in the coming year is shared with the world.

Clockwise from left: brainstorming at Travel Hack events in Seoul, Franklin, Běijīng and Stuttgart

BEST IN TRAVEL 2019 JUDGING PANEL

• Piera Chen

Piera is a travel writer who divides her time between Hong Kong (hometown), Taiwan and Vancouver when not on the road. She has authored over a dozen travel guides and contributed to just as many travel-related titles. Piera has a BA in literature from Pomona College, in California. Her early life was peppered with trips to Taiwan and China to visit relatives, and then to Southeast Asia where her father was working. But it was during her first trip to Europe that dawn broke. She remembers fresh off a flight, looking around her in Rome, thinking, 'I want to be doing this everyday.' And she has.

• Bailey Freeman

As Lonely Planet's Destination Editor for South America & Antarctica, Bailey Freeman has commissioned and managed the content for 45 countries and written pieces for lonelyplanet.com, the Lonely Planet US magazine, and coffee-table titles like *Secret Marvels of the World*. Her work has led her on many adventures throughout Latin America and the Caribbean, her areas of speciality, and she calls Nashville, Tennessee, home.

• Tony Wheeler

Tony was one of the founders of Lonely Planet and wrote many of the early guidebooks. Recently he's contributed to *The Travel Atlas*, *Epic Drives of the World* and *The Cities Book*. In 2017 he spent four months driving along the Silk Road from Bangkok to London and his recent travels have taken him to Rohingya refugee camps in Bangladesh and to the Italian colonial architecture of Asmara in Eritrea.

• Kia Abdullah

Kia Abdullah is an author and travel writer based in London, UK. She has written two novels and contributed to *The Guardian*, *The New York Times*, BBC and Channel 4 News. Kia is a Lonely Planet Trailblazer and the founding editor of outdoor travel blog Atlas & Boots. She has visited more than 50 countries in pursuit of the world's best outdoor activities and believes nature is the best antidote to the stresses of modern life.

• Andrea Schulte-Peevers

Born and raised in Germany and educated in London and at UCLA, Andrea has travelled the distance to the moon and back in her visits to some 75 countries. She has earned her living as a professional travel writer for over two decades and authored or contributed to nearly 100 Lonely Planet titles as well as newspapers, magazines and websites around the world. She also works as a travel consultant, translator and editor. Andrea's destination expertise is especially strong when it comes to Germany, Dubai and the UAE, Crete and the Caribbean Islands. She makes her home in Berlin.

• Martin Heng

Martin left England in 1987 and travelled for a decade before migrating to Australia to start a family. He has worked for Lonely Planet since 1999 in many different roles, including seven years as Editorial Manager, until a road accident in 2010 left him a quadriplegic. As Lonely Planet's Accessible Travel Manager he has published several accessible travel titles, including the world's largest collection of online resources for accessible travel. He has become a regular speaker at accessible travel conferences around the world.

ACKNOWLEDGEMENTS

PUBLISHED IN 2018 BY LONELY PLANET GLOBAL LIMITED

CRN 554153
www.lonelyplanet.com
978 1 78701 765 8
© Lonely Planet 2018
© Photographs as indicated 2018
Printed in Singapore
1 2 3 4 5 6 7 8 9 10

MANAGING DIRECTOR, PUBLISHING Piers Pickard
ASSOCIATE PUBLISHER Robin Barton
COMMISSIONING EDITOR Dora Ball
ASSISTANT EDITOR Christina Webb
ART DIRECTION Daniel Di Paolo
LAYOUT DESIGNER Tina García
EDITORS Andrea Dobbin, Nick Mee
IMAGE RESEARCHER Tania Cagnoni, Julie Selby
CARTOGRAPHY Michael Garrett, Wayne Murphy
PRINT PRODUCTION Nigel Longuet
COVER IMAGE Guitar photographer © Shutterstock
THANKS TO Barbara Di Castro, Tom Davis, Jon
Dicus, Victor Huckabee, Katie Johnson, Laura
Lindsay, Dr Doug Marmion, Flora MacQueen,
Jacob Rhoades

WRITTEN BY Louise Bastock, Joe Bindloss, Greg
Bloom, Cristian Bonetto, Alex Butler, Daniel
James Clarke, Megan Eaves, Bailey Freeman,
Ethan Gelber, Imogen Hall, Tom Hall, Paul Harding,
Damian Harper, Trent Holden, Stephen Lioy, James
Kay, Tom Masters, AnneMarie McCarthy, Carolyn
McCarthy, Maria McKenzie, Lorna Parkes, Matt
Phillips, Brandon Presser, Brendan Sainsbury,
Andrea Schulte-Peevers, Regis St Louis, Sarah
Stocking, Branislava Vladisavljevic, Tasmin Waby,
Jenny Walker, Donna Wheeler, Neil Wilson

STAY IN TOUCH lonelyplanet.com/contact

AUSTRALIA The Malt Store, Level 3, 551 Swanston
St, Carlton, Victoria 3053; 03 8379 8000

IRELAND Digital Depot, Roe Lane (off Thomas
St), Dublin 8, D08 TCV4

USA 124 Linden St, Oakland, CA 94607
510 250 6400

UK 240 Blackfriars Rd, London SE1 8NW
020 3771 5100

Although the authors and Lonely Planet have
taken all reasonable care in preparing this book,
we make no warranty about the accuracy or
completeness of its content and, to the maximum
extent permitted, disclaim all liability from its use.

Paper in this book is certified against the
Forest Stewardship Council™ standards.
FSC™ promotes environmentally responsible,
socially beneficial and economically viable
management of the world's forests.

MAKE IT HAPPEN

Plan your 2019 travel with Lonely Planet

China · Europe · USA · Nepal

Denmark · Seattle · Africa · Croatia · Mexico · Morocco

Ready to go after reading this year's Best in Travel list?
We've got guidebooks covering each of the top destinations.